BLACK MARKET ADOPTION

BLACK MARKET
ADOPTION

—————— $ ——————

AND THE SALE OF CHILDREN
BY ELAINE LANDAU

Franklin Watts
New York / London / Toronto / Sydney / 1990
An Impact Book

Photographs courtesy of:
UPI/Bettmann Newsphotos: pp. 11, 14, 66,
69, 74, 80, 91; AP/Wide World Photos:
pp. 15 (both), 17, 21, 22, 23, 28, 56, 58.

Library of Congress Cataloging-in-Publication Data

Landau, Elaine.
Black market adoption and the sale of children / by Elaine Landau.
p.   cm.—(An Impact book)
Includes bibliographical references.
Summary: Examines the problems of illegal adoption and surrogate
motherhood and the tragedies which often result from them. Offers
solutions to the ethical and legal dilemmas caused by this form of
commerce.
ISBN 0-531-10914-3
1. Adoption—United States—Corrupt practices—Juvenile
literature. [1. Adoption—Corrupt practices. 2. Surrogate
motherhood—Moral and ethical aspects.]   I. Title.
HV875.55.L36   1990
364.1′8—dc20   89-39639   CIP   AC

$

CONTENTS

BLACK MARKET ADOPTION

FOR NORMAN

ONE

"BEATEN INTO UNCONSCIOUSNESS"

On November 2, 1987, New York City police officers responded to a call that brought them to the home of lawyer Joel Steinberg and his common-law wife Hedda Nussbaum. There, in the squalid and disheveled upstairs apartments, the police found two small children—a six-year-old girl and a seventeen-month-old boy. The little girl, Lisa, had been beaten into unconsciousness while the toddler, Travis (then known as Mitchell), had been tied to a chair as he sat on the floor in his own excrement. Travis's small body was encrusted with dirt, and he had been drinking a bottle of spoiled milk.[1]

After rushing Lisa to nearby St. Vincent's Hospital for emergency treatment, the officers returned to Steinberg's residence to escort Steinberg and Nussbaum down to the West Tenth Street police station for further questioning. At first Steinberg had tried to thwart the officers' attempt to reenter the apartment, initially claiming that he was sleeping and then that he was on the telephone with the hospital. However, once he relented and the police had an opportunity to survey the premises, they asked Steinberg where the young boy slept. Steinberg simply answered, "There," and pointed to the floor.[2]

Despite the intensive efforts by doctors and other hospital staff, Lisa died on November 5th, several days after being hospitalized. Lisa, who had been referred to as "our sleeping beauty" by hospital nurses, had never regained consciousness.

"Lisa Steinberg has expired," said Barbara Fran, spokeswoman for St. Vincent's Hospital. "The case is now under the jurisdiction of the medical examiner."[3] Following an autopsy, the medical examiner's office concluded that Lisa had been killed as the result of repeated blows to her head and body in what had been termed a homicidal beating. Immediately following the child's death, Joel Steinberg was charged with second-degree murder, manslaughter, and endangering the life of a child.

Little Lisa's story actually began six years ago when a nineteen-year-old teenager named Michelle Launders gave birth to her on the morning of May 14, 1981, at the New York Infirmary-Beekman Downtown Hospital. As an unmarried teenager, Ms. Launders felt that her child would be best off if she put the baby up for adoption. Ms. Launders told the press: "I was not married. I was nineteen, and I felt that there were things which she deserved that I could not provide her."[4]

Michelle Launders had been referred to attorney Joel Steinberg by her doctor, the late Michael Bergman, a Long Island obstetrician who himself died following a prolonged illness only weeks before young Lisa's untimely death. Throughout her pregnancy and

*The small white coffin of adoption victim
Lisa Steinberg was an unforgettable
sight to the many who grieved her death.*

the birth of her daughter, Ms. Launders had believed that her physician had only been trying to be helpful. In fact, during the last three months of her pregnancy, she had even moved in with the doctor's receptionist.

Michelle Launders paid Joel Steinberg five hundred dollars to ensure that Lisa would be given a proper home. Herself a devout Catholic, Ms. Launders testified in Manhattan Surrogates Court that it had been her understanding that her infant daughter would be placed with a professional Roman Catholic family. As her attorney Anthony Cornachio told the press: "She was told that her child would have opportunities from this middle-income family that she could never give the child herself. . . . She was told that the child will never want for anything."[5]

Ms. Launders further testified that Steinberg had assured her that her baby was to be adopted by "a couple in Manhattan, that one was an attorney and that he [Steinberg] wanted to know who the father was, what religion he was in, because the adoptive parents had a right to know."[6]

Michelle Launders also pointed out that Lisa's medical records had been changed. Steinberg had been listed as the baby's father, although this information was false. When asked in court if Steinberg had ever told her that he intended to keep the baby himself, Ms. Launders loudly answered, "Never."[7]

Following Lisa's death, the Steinberg residence was described by a city social worker (in an affidavit filed in Family Court) as being "filthy and disorganized." Lisa and the seventeen-month-old boy who lived there with her, it was stated in the document, "were repeatedly exposed to incidents of domestic violence." The social worker said that the young boy was "soaked with urine and was wearing a diaper that appeared to be days old."[8]

Michelle Launders had seen her baby only for seconds before the child was given over to Steinberg. As it turned out, Steinberg and Nussbaum never legally adopted Lisa. She and Travis had been secured by deceiving both children's natural mothers. In both cases the young natural mothers had been told that their babies were being placed with outstanding families.

On a news program Michelle Launders had heard about the little girl who had been brutally abused. When she learned that it was her own daughter who had been killed, her reaction was one of shock and revulsion. In disbelief she told the press, "Why did they murder my baby? If I had wanted my baby murdered, I would have had an abortion."[9]

Nicole Smigiel, the little boy's natural mother, had given birth to her son when she was only sixteen. At the time she had given up Travis for adoption on the assumption that he'd be going to a good home. When Ms. Smigiel learned of her son's actual fate, she dropped out of her sophomore year at Loyola College in Baltimore, Maryland, and returned home to Long Island, New York, to live with her parents and raise her son.

As Nicole Smigiel's lawyer, Anthony Barbiero, stated, "The baby is going to be treated as a baby who has come home to his mother after a long time, with a lot of love."[10]

As a result of Lisa Steinberg's death and the phony adoptions of her and the male child living with Steinberg, Manhattan prosecutors sent out dozens of sub-

*Michelle Launders, Lisa's natural mother,
arrives for the funeral of the daughter she
gave up so that the child could have a better life
than what Launders felt she could give her.*

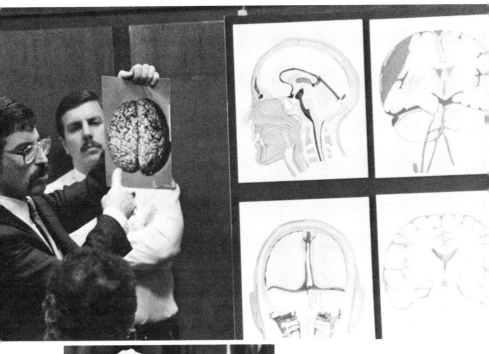

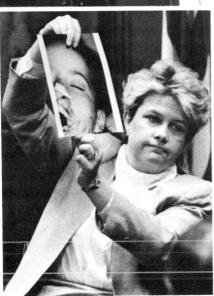

Evidence was offered at the trial of Joel Steinberg for the death of the illegally adopted Lisa that showed she suffered brain damage (top) and bruises that suggested child abuse (bottom).

poenas to local doctors, lawyers, and hospitals in an attempt to establish Joel Steinberg's ties to a black market adoption ring. As Manhattan District Attorney Robert Morgenthau told the press: "We're going to look at the so-called adoptions of these two children. If that leads us to other improper adoptions, we will take appropriate action."[11]

The outcome of the district attorney's investigation revealed that a number of doctors and attorneys are making hundreds of thousands of dollars selling babies. One of the lawyers is believed to have sold over two hundred babies in a single year. According to the investigation report, an underground black market exists in New York City, and loopholes in the adoption laws permit illegal placements to occur. The going rate for a healthy white baby ranged from $75,000 to $100,000.[12]

The sale of human beings in the United States was supposedly outlawed with the abolition of slavery following the Civil War. Yet there is evidence to suggest that the sale of healthy white infants thrives in America today. Black market adoption can be a financially rewarding enterprise for modern-day baby merchants. The people who lose in these dealings are the children, their natural parents, and often innocent adoptive parents who at times become unwittingly involved with unscrupulous baby dealers.

Lisa Steinberg was the child victim of a shady adoption scheme. Unfortunately it cost her her life. Her "adoptive" brother Travis was returned to his biological mother as the result of the publicity and the investigation which surrounded Lisa's death.

In this instance Travis's biological mother, Nicole Smigiel, was fortunate. Michelle Launders, Lisa's

Nicole Smigiel shows off her son Travis
after getting temporary custody of the child
found in the same apartment as Lisa Steinberg.

natural mother, was not. In fact, Nicole wrote the following note to Michelle following Lisa's burial.

Dear Michelle,

I pray for you and your little angel, because without her, I would not have my little angel. You are forever in my heart.

> *With deepest feelings,*
> *Nicole*[13]

Travis's story had a happy ending. He had begun a new life with his biological mother and her family. Travis was lucky. But unfortunately many young victims of black market adoptions do not fare as well.

TWO

ADOPTIONS

It's an American dream. Boy meets girl. They fall in love and marry. Out of their joy-filled union a child is born. And so another happy family is created.

Although many individuals may envision the above as an important part of their future, it will never be a reality for millions of Americans. According to the National Center for Health Statistics, as of 1985, one out of every nine couples of childbearing age will experience difficulties in either conceiving or maintaining a pregnancy.[1]

A study cited in the *Ladies' Home Journal* indicated that while in 1938 only one American couple in twenty was infertile, today that number has risen to one in seven.[2] The increase in infertility has been attributed to such factors as environmental pollution, as well as to the fact that currently many women are postponing marriage and motherhood until they have established themselves professionally.[3]

Often couples who put off having children later find the would-be mother's age to be a problem. In the last two decades, the number of women having their first child between the ages of thirty and thirty-four has quadrupled. According to Dr. Brian Cohen, an infertility specialist from Dallas, Texas:

> *From an international point of view the American woman is the most dynamic, most accomplished in the world. She also shows the highest incidence of postponing childbearing and problems associated with infertility. We pay a price for waiting.*[4]

In actuality there are approximately three million American couples and singles who desperately want a baby, but who have found it nearly impossible to obtain one.[5] Due to the availability of birth control and abortion, considerably fewer unwanted children have been born than in the past.

In addition more relaxed social attitudes have encouraged unmarried mothers to keep their babies. Today nearly 96 percent of the single mothers in the United States raise their own children.[6]

As a result, more than ever before, people are turning to adoption in order to start a family of their own. The type of adoption that we are most familiar with is known as agency adoption. In an agency adoption a state-licensed adoption agency acts as an intermediary between the child's natural mother and the adoptive parent(s). In an agency adoption the agency is responsible for the careful screening of all prospective adoptive parents who apply for their service.

Although efforts to educate young people
(like the above Planned Parenthood comic book)
have resulted in fewer unwanted children
being born, now there are also fewer
babies available for adoption.

*Some people believe the availability
of abortion keeps many children from
being born who would later be adopted.*

Unmarried mothers are not stigmatized as they once were. These young women are participating in a YWCA program for unemployed teenage mothers.

Approaching a reputable agency to secure a child is perhaps the most traditional and safest route to adoption. However, prospective adoptive parents desiring healthy white infants may soon find that their goal isn't easily attained.

For one thing, "ideal" or "perfect" babies of this type are not plentiful or even readily available. In the text *The Penguin Adoption Handbook,* the director of a small adoption agency in the Midwest described the situation: "We get four hundred inquiries a year, and ninety-five percent of those families would provide perfectly fine homes for the children."[7]

However, the problem lies in the fact that the agency has only about thirty healthy babies annually available for placement. So as a result each year the agency receives sufficient inquiry calls from qualified potential adoptive parents to keep its waiting list filled for the next thirteen years!

Roger Toogood, executive director of the Children's Home Society of Minnesota, estimated in 1986 that there are approximately a hundred couples waiting for each white infant available through traditional agency channels.[8]

Due to today's dramatic shortage of infants and babies, many traditional agencies have rechanneled their energies toward finding suitable parents for teenagers, older children who have spent most of their lives in various foster homes, children who are either mentally, physically, or emotionally handicapped, or children of racial minorities. And although these young people are as deserving of a loving home as any child, often couples are interested only in adopting white infants.

However, even couples who are willing to adopt a minority group baby may soon learn that they'll face numerous obstacles in their search for an infant. As Peter Winkler, Director of Adoption Services for the state of New York, described the adoption predicament in a *Cosmopolitan* magazine article: "True, there are more minority babies than white available, but healthy infants of any racial group are still scarce. Also, we try to place children in homes where the parents have similar racial and ethnic backgrounds. I'm not saying a white couple in this country could never adopt a black infant, for example, but it doesn't happen often."[9]

The director of a New York adoption agency underscored these sentiments: "We might give a single woman a twelve- or thirteen-year-old or a retarded child, but that's all. We have scores of well-heeled, young professional couples who can give a baby everything. Why should we even consider placing an infant with a single woman who may have a struggle to find decent day care?"[10]

Often many traditional agencies adhere strictly to guidelines which have been criticized by some as being overly rigid. The following requirements are a sample of the expectations that prospective adoptive parents must meet in order to be taken on as clients by a traditional adoption agency.[11]

a. Preferred clients tend to be stable couples who have been married for a number of years. Although in recent years a previous divorce has become more acceptable, most agencies will need to carefully examine what went wrong in the past relationship to try to ensure that it doesn't occur again.

b. Preferred clients tend to be somewhat affluent. Ideally, the family should be able to afford material comforts and live comfortably on solely the husband's salary. It is generally expected that the wife will either stop working or work part-time to enable her to devote sufficient time and attention to making a home for the family.

c. The good health of both adoptive parents is of primary importance. Obesity, physical disabilities, and chronic diseases are frowned upon.

d. Both the husband and wife should be under forty years of age. Although applicants beyond that age may be able to convince the agency that they are presently vigorous, active, and in good health, those faced with the responsibility of placing the child may still doubt the prospective parents' ability to raise an active teenager sixteen years from now.

e. A good educational background is considered a plus. Applicants with college degrees are seen as especially desirable.

f. Preferred clients are members of a church or synagogue or have a firm moral philosophy to impart to the child.

g. Couples wishing to adopt a healthy white infant should be able to provide verification from a physician that they are biologically infertile.

Many couples and individuals who wish to adopt do not meet all of the above requirements or the additional specifications which may be imposed on them by some traditional agencies. Although it may be easier to adopt an older or minority group child or one who is physically, mentally, or emotionally handicapped, often prospective adoptive parents are not interested in doing so.

Frequently couples are also alienated by the stringent requirements imposed on applicants by traditional adoption agencies. One New York adoptive mother described her interview at one such adoption agency as follows: "We came out of there feeling resentful that millions of people—many of them less responsible than we—were having babies, and we were being grilled."[12]

Still, William Pierce, Ph.D., president of the National Committee for Adoption in Washington, D.C., supports the cautious attitude which is often characteristic of traditional adoption agencies. According to Dr. Pierce, "One man's restrictions are another man's standards. If God wants to give somebody a baby, that's God's responsibility. But when society places agencies in a God-like role, then those agencies have to find the very best family for the child. When there is a surplus of couples who are optimal in every way, why should a child have to settle for second best?"[13]

After being turned down by a traditional adoption agency or being placed on a lengthy waiting list, some individuals may choose to explore another type of adoption known as independent adoption.

Independent adoption, which is sometimes referred to as the "gray market," is adoption arranged by either the child's biological mother or a middle person such as her doctor or an attorney. Theoretically the costs to an adoptive couple will entail only the biological mother's medical expenses, which should be thoroughly documented by itemized bills, as well as a reasonable fee paid to the attorney.

Technically gray market adoption is legal. Although it's against the law to buy or sell a baby or any human being, the matter of fees for adoption re-

This couple, sixtieth in line, waits for their chance—the following day!—to submit an application to adopt a baby.

mains a hazy area. Therefore, in a gray market adoption, if the attorney involved collects only a reasonable fee for services in arranging the adoption and nothing more, he or she is still acting within the law. Paying expenses is legal; buying babies is not.[14]

Historically, most state laws permitting independent adoption originated to allow an unwed mother who personally knew of a couple who wished to adopt her baby to do so. Ideally, the pregnant woman would work out the details with the couple, while both sides would retain attorneys simply to complete the necessary forms and paperwork required by the courts.

However, in most cases the young woman who became pregnant did not know of prospective adoptive couples. In addition the pregnant females usually did not have an adequate means of finding them on their own. Instead they were often assisted by their doctor or an attorney who helped to place the baby by acting as a connection between the biological mother and the adoptive parents.

Those in favor of independent adoption argue that it allows babies to be placed with couples who can provide good homes though they may have been turned down by a traditional adoption agency for what might seem like a superficial reason. Other couples, who grew tired of having their names remain on a lengthy waiting list, may have turned to independent adoption hoping to find a quicker way to become parents.

At times the baby's biological mother may prefer independent adoption over agency adoption because it affords her an opportunity to either meet the adoptive parents or obtain information about them through the attorney. Approximately half of the twenty or twenty-five thousand babies adopted each year are placed without the help of licensed nonprofit adoption agencies.[15]

Although many private placement adoptions provide infants with caring parents, the lack of agency oversight and limited statutory guidance provide an opportunity for abuse. State-licensed adoption agencies tend to be adamantly opposed to independent adoptions, which are out of their control. They are largely in agreement that adoptions of this nature are undesirable and may prove to be problematic or even dangerous for the infants involved. As Jeffrey Rosenberg, director for adoption services of the National Committee for Adoption, stated, "It is not a system for protecting the interests of the child."[16]

Adoptions are regulated by the state, and there is a good deal of variation in the adoption laws of different states. In some states independent adoptions have been banned entirely. Therefore, a couple who has been turned down by a traditional agency and lives in a state where independent adoptions are illegal has the option of either moving to a state where the practice is permitted or having an independent adoption arranged for them in a state without a residency requirement. At times the latter alternative has resulted in unsavory alliances with unscrupulous baby merchants.

Regardless of what state the adoption takes place in, a study of the adopting family by a licensed professional social worker must be completed and submitted to the court in order for the adoption to be formalized legally. These studies are done routinely for the clients of traditional state-licensed agencies as part of the service offered to prospective adoptive parents. But independent adoptions cannot be finalized anywhere in the United States until a court has seen evidence that a comparable study was completed and that the adoptive family has been approved.

It is at this juncture that couples most fear losing the child whom they hope will be theirs. And those who are not approved may be forced to face that disappointing reality.

However, in most cases of independent adoption, a child remains in the home of the adoptive parents despite a possible negative report. This is largely due to the fact that the home investigation is not conducted until the adoptive family has already obtained custody. As the courts are reluctant to remove a baby from its adoptive home, the investigations completed by assigned social workers tend to be somewhat superficial.

Mary Beth Seader of the National Committee for Adoption in Washington, D.C., has publicly stated that independent adoptive parents aren't always screened adequately or at all. As she stated to the press, "If you've got money, you can get a child."[17]

Courts will often tend to leave an adoptive child in a less than perfect home rather than remove the infant to have it placed elsewhere. However, some people do feel that a child less than a year old would be better off adjusting to new parents than living out a life sentence of abuse.

The courts' attitude is perhaps best reflected by the following case cited by Nancy C. Baker in her book *Baby Selling: The Scandal of Black Market Adoptions*. In this instance a social worker assigned to investigate the potential adoptive parents in an independent adoption found the couple to be woefully inadequate and unsuitable as care givers. They had brutally abused their adopted infant and had even broken several of the child's bones.

The social worker came to court armed with police reports and other documentation which served to positively verify that both the husband and wife were guilty of child abuse. However, regardless of the proof submitted to him, the judge still refused to take the child from its home. Instead, he went ahead with the paperwork and completed the adoption.[18]

A similar occurrence took place in Portland, Oregon, where a psychotic couple were able to adopt a child through independent adoption. Although their mental state would have been quickly discovered if a preplacement study had been done by a state-licensed agency, only a cursory investigation had been completed because the child was already in its new home. As a result, nearly six years passed before the parents' mental problems came to light.[19]

Still another case happened in the South, where a couple whose biological child had been removed from their home due to neglect and abuse were still permitted to adopt a newborn. As might be expected, they abused their adopted baby as well.[20]

Although most individuals adopting independently act quickly to finalize the transaction in order to protect their claim to the child, this is not always the case. In fact there is no officially designated state or city board responsible for following up on a couple who take a baby from its biological mother and promise to adopt.

As Jane Edwards, executive director of the Spence Chapin Services to Families and Children, a traditional agency which does extensive evaluations of adoptive families stated in the newspaper, *New York*

Newsday, "There is no supervision, no state agency that monitors families to see whether in fact the children are actually adopted."[21] So in actuality some would-be independent adoptions never even reach a court-room.

A third type of adoption which in some ways resembles gray market adoption is called black market adoption. In both these instances an independent third party negotiates the child's exchange between the biological mother and the adoptive parents. However, in black market adoption the costs to the adoptive parents can be astronomical.

At a hearing of the Senate Subcommittee on Children and Youth, one witness who had personally tried to adopt a baby outside of traditional agency channels told the panel, "Some of the lawyers I've spoken to have made such statements as, 'If you really wanted this child, you'd find a way to pay my fee.' Another lawyer said, 'Take it or leave it. I have five other couples.' "[22]

In black market adoption babies are matched up with prospective parents who can raise the asking price. The price tag placed on any individual baby may vary according to the child's hereditary makeup. Often to collect a more substantial fee, baby brokers will deliberately distort facts about the infant's background to make the child appear more desirable.

For example, the prospective adoptive parents may be told that the baby they are getting is the illegitimate offspring of a college honor student and her married professor. In actuality the baby's mother could have been a high school dropout, while her boyfriend, the baby's father, might be someone who is continually in trouble with the law.

In black market adoption desirable couples are not

sought to provide homes for unwanted babies, but rather couples fervently search for desirable babies. They are looking for children of the highest caliber, babies with backgrounds that spell potential and promise; to many people, this means babies who genetically possess the most valued physical and mental attributes.

In an independent adoption the child is taken from the biological mother within days of its birth and placed with the adoptive parents. In a traditional agency adoption, the agency assumes custody of the child immediately following birth and then places the infant in foster care for as long as necessary while the prospective adoptive parents are chosen and screened. The important difference is that in agency adoption the state-licensed organization specifically chooses the parents, while in black market adoption, the adoptive parents pick and purchase the child.

THREE

THE BLACK MARKET

Black market adoption is a booming American enterprise. Depending on the child's seeming desirability to his or her prospective adoptive parents, prices for babies can range anywhere from between $4,000 and $40,000.[1] And in some instances infant price tags have grown even larger.

As one witness, Sharon Horner, a representative of the Adoptive Parents Group of Philadelphia, testified before a Senate Subcommittee on Children and Youth: "Some of the lawyers I've spoken to have made such statements as, 'My price is $10,000 plus hospital expenses. Had you called three months ago, it would have been $7,000, but you understand about supply and demand.' "[2]

At the same hearings, the Deputy District Attorney for Los Angeles County, Richard A. Moss, described to the committee a case in which an attorney had set up an organization through which infants were sold for upwards of ten thousand dollars each. In addition the attorney had tried to convince young women to conceive children who could be sold for adoption. The Deputy District Attorney produced records of correspondence which indicated that on two separate occasions European women were offered a warm weather vacation plus a cash payment if they would become pregnant and then turn over the child.[3]

At the hearing Fred Francis, an investigative reporter for Miami TV WTVJ, screened several documentaries he had filmed on black market adoption. According to Mr. Francis, the baby merchants set up homes for pregnant women which were actually little more than "warehouses for unwed mothers." Following their birth, the infants were sold to individuals who could meet the asking price. The reporter likened the situation to slavery. "I see no difference. You're talking about passing human beings across state lines for high profits."[4]

Today black market profiteers run lucrative businesses built on greed and the exploitation of often innocent and well-meaning individuals. Investigative reporter and author Lynne McTaggart described the process in an article in the *Saturday Review:* "As in any other business, baby brokers have been able to turn a healthy profit through the shrewd exercising of rather sophisticated merchandising principles, the most fundamental of which is that limited supply and increased demand boost the going rates. They have set up national and international importing networks. They offer insurance policies and 'package' deals. They've invented elaborate come-ons and gimmickry designed to induce pregnant girls to give up their babies. There is warehousing, bidding, bargaining, and price tags of ten thousand dollars or more."[5]

Black market adoption is primarily characterized by an abuse of power and a lack of safeguards that typify traditional agency adoption. Ideally, in independent adoption, separate attorneys would be retained by both the biological mother and the prospective adoptive parents to complete the necessary paperwork required by the courts. However, in black market adoption usually one attorney controls the entire process. These lawyers are not merely acting as intermediaries; instead they are actively involved in the baby business, keeping up-to-the-minute lists on available newborns and prospective parents. They serve more as illegal brokers than as legal counsels. Infant entrepreneurs operate within a broadly open seller's market. In many instances they have become the only means through which a childless couple can obtain a healthy white American-born baby within a reasonable period of time.

Why have baby merchants been so successful in gathering a healthy supply of desirable infants? One reason is that they've searched more aggressively for unwed expectant mothers than traditional adoption agencies. According to Lynne McTaggart in her article, "The Booming Adoption Racket," "They enlist the help of abortion clinics, hospitals, pregnancy-testing services, and abortion hotlines; they work with finders and other attorneys in the United States and foreign countries, they arrange quid-pro-quo deals with doctors, trading obstetrical business for referrals."[6]

Baby merchants work hard to make their efforts enticing to expectant mothers. The packages they design may appear especially appealing to young pregnant women facing a difficult financial dilemma. Usually a baby merchant will immediately assure the mother-to-be that her room, board, and medical expenses will be paid for. Often the expectant mother will also be promised a modest amount of spending money, funds for maternity clothes, as well as a few dollars for entertainment. Such items are freely offered at no cost to the middle person, since these expenses are passed on to the prospective adoptive parents.

In attempting to persuade a pregnant woman to relinquish her baby, the baby merchants are generally careful to avoid any of the intrusive or judgmental questions that are often posed to pregnant unmarried women by traditional adoption agencies. Frequently the black market profiteer will instead stress the extremely private nature of the alternative offered, assuring the pregnant woman involved that her confidentiality will be guarded. The baby merchant's ultimate goal is to secure the desired commodity—a healthy white, salable infant. He or she will be careful not to do anything which might encourage a pregnant woman to go elsewhere.

Couples who desperately want a family may feel they have to cooperate with the baby merchant. Such prospective adoptive parents have to be prepared to come up with a hefty sum to obtain a baby and must realize that some of their transactions need to be conducted in cash. Although most states allow adoptive parents to pay for the biological mother's medical expenses and reasonable living costs, neither the birth mother nor the attorney involved may legally receive either monetary rewards or valuables in return for handing over the child.

As a result couples who pursue black market adoption may find themselves forced to lie to the authorities about undeclared cash payments made to the attorney during the adoption procedure. These prospective adoptive parents may also have to provide untrue statements regarding the moneys exchanged both to the social worker conducting the home investigation as well as to the court for its documentation. If the adoptive parents live in an area where independent adoption has been outlawed, they'll have to swear that they reside at a fraudulent address provided for them by the attorney. However, usually the couples go along with the prescribed terms and ask few questions. They believe that their alternatives are scarce.

But no matter how the adoptive parents try to justify their actions, buying a baby usually takes on an unsavory flavor. Often final payments may be furtively exchanged in hospital parking lots or between the would-be father and the attorney in a men's room near the hospital nursery.

Since infants are at such a premium, baby merchants may aim a variety of manipulative tactics at expectant mothers as well. It is not uncommon for pregnant teenagers to be offered substantial bribes for their babies. New mothers are often otherwise coerced into surrendering their infants for adoption as well.

For example, when handling private adoptions of this nature, attorneys may arrange for the biological mother to appear in court before a judge in order to surrender her child. In this way the usual thirty-day grace period during which a natural mother may change her mind and keep her baby is automatically forfeited. Her decision to surrender the infant and relinquish custody becomes immediately binding and irreversible.

In addition, although the pregnant women are generally told that all their expenses will be covered until after the child's birth, some attorneys may ask them to sign a contract holding them legally liable for all expenses incurred if they change their mind and choose to keep the baby prior to the court adoption. With the considerable medical costs involved in childbirth and after care, this stipulation might easily place a woman with only minimal funds in an extremely difficult position.

At times pregnant women who become involved with baby merchants may be threatened, deliberately given misinformation about their rights, or at best receive highly biased counseling. The situation may become especially tense for young, naive females or foreign-born women who do not fully comprehend the language.

In her book *The Baby Brokers,* Lynne McTaggart describes the sad plight of a pregnant woman who was flown from Europe to the United States by an attorney after she had answered an ad in a local newspaper.[7] By arranging for her to give birth on United States soil, the woman's newborn would automatically become a United States citizen. In this way, all the red tape and bureaucracy involving immigration and naturalization could be successfully avoided. It was an efficient way to procure a much desired commodity.

During her stay in the United States, the expectant mother often felt isolated and alone. Many times she wondered if she were doing the right thing, but she spoke little English, and there was no one for her to discuss her feelings with.

The woman gave birth to a baby boy whom she barely saw. Before her flight home, she was taken to the attorney's office where she was told to sign three sets of incomplete legal documents. She was not told what she was signing. Nor was she given any information about her son's new adoptive home, as she had been promised.

After signing the papers, the woman was driven to a court, where she swore before a judge that she was permanently relinquishing custody of her baby. Since the legal proceedings were conducted in English, she understood very little of it. En route to the courthouse an associate of the attorney who spoke her language stressed that she was not to mention the newspaper ad through which she had originally connected with their operation.

The woman returned to Europe without ever meeting her son's adoptive parents or seeing the wonderful home which she thought she'd be bringing him to. Looking back on her experience, she believes that the child she gave birth to in America was sold. As she sobbingly related, "There was nothing human about my dealings. . . . It was all a commercial business, that's what I saw in all of them."[8]

FOUR

BIRTH MOTHERS

In *Baby Selling: The Scandal of Black Market Adoption,* Nancy C. Baker cites the case of Isabel, a nineteen-year-old from Guatemala City who became pregnant as the result of a gang rape involving four men.[1] Being unmarried and coming from a strict religious home, Isabel feared that her condition might embarrass her family. She decided to leave the country to have the baby and subsequently entered the United States as an illegal alien.

Isabel managed to find work in Los Angeles doing light domestic chores for a middle-class family. She noticed early on that the woman for whom she worked appeared overly interested in the fact that she was pregnant and alone. Her employer urged Isabel to give up the baby for adoption. The woman continually stressed that she and her husband had helped a number of unwed mothers who had happily parted with their children in this manner.

Isabel listened patiently to what her employer said but found herself unable to go along with what was being asked of her. Despite the fact that she was alone in a strange country without friends or her family, Isabel still wasn't prepared to give up her baby.

Several months later when Isabel went into labor, her employer took her to an exclusive private hospital whose fees Isabel would be unable to pay. While at the hospital, Isabel was asked to sign a number of papers. Isabel did as she was told, but as she had only a limited knowledge of English, she was unable to understand the documents.

Isabel stayed in the hospital for more than three weeks, although she didn't know why such a lengthy hospitalization had been necessary. She also found it strange that she had not been permitted to see her baby during the time that she remained in the hospital. Throughout this period Isabel had believed that her child was being well cared for by the staff in the hospital's nursery. She had no idea that the infant had already been placed with adoptive parents.

When Isabel learned the truth, she called the lawyer who had had her sign the papers and demanded to know her child's whereabouts. Isabel went to the adoptive parents' home and retrieved the baby, but she soon learned that the adoptive parents were not about to part with the infant easily.

At first they tried to bribe Isabel into giving up her baby. They bought her clothes, took her out to the movies, and offered her substantial sums of money. Their lawyer told Isabel that her United States citizenship would be a certainty if she cooperated.

When those tactics proved unsuccessful, Isabel began to receive threatening anonymous phone calls.

The caller reminded Isabel that children can easily have accidents and that something might happen to her baby.

After substantial pressure Isabel gave in to the adoptive parents' demands. She explained, "I would rather that my baby be safe somewhere else than be in danger with me. So I signed the papers."[2]

However, within a short period of time, Isabel found that she was unable to live with her decision. She loved her baby and wanted the child back. Isabel felt so strongly about the matter that she decided to risk deportation and seek legal help in going to court to regain custody of her child.

Isabel contacted the Long Beach Legal Aid Society in California where she was assigned an attorney to represent her. But Isabel's struggle to have her child returned to her proved to be a difficult battle to win. By this time the court was concerned only with whether or not the final adoption papers had actually been signed by the child's natural mother. As Isabel had signed these final release forms previously, the judge ruled that her child's adoption was binding and would not be overturned by the court.

Ms. Ramirez, Isabel's attorney, explained the circumstances as follows: "My client claimed that she signed the papers, but didn't understand the legal consequences because she didn't speak English and the translator for the Adoptions Department explained the procedure to her in such a way that she could believe this was only the first part of the adoption and she would later have a chance to go to court and change her mind."[3]

Unfortunately the fact that Isabel was a maid may have weighed negatively in the judge's determination of where the baby would be best off. As Isabel's attorney went on to explain: "In addition, the judge was interested in selecting the best home for the baby. The couple has a lot of money and my client is employed as a domestic. The judge can take into consideration the economic status of the adoptive parents as opposed to the natural parent and say, 'Well, in view of this, I don't think the child should be returned because it's going to be living with a person who's basically a maid.' "[4]

The judge's decision may have also been influenced by the language barriers presented by the case. According to Ms. Ramirez, "When you have someone translating on the stand, you lose a lot of the punch, especially when the translator is a man. No matter what was said, it didn't carry the emotional weight of Isabel's own words."[5]

Isabel lost her baby. Following the trial, she moved, leaving no forwarding address because she still feared deportation by the immigration authorities. Isabel believes that she was the victim of a baby-selling ring.

Naive young pregnant women are often the prime targets of baby merchants. In many instances young white females from middle- and working-class homes are considered their most valuable finds. One such incident involved a pregnant seventeen-year-old high school dropout from a Pennsylvania coal mining town.[6]

Seeing few options available to her, the young woman responded to an advertisement she had noticed in a local newspaper. Through a telephone conversation the baby merchant had instructed the girl to fly to Baton Rouge, Louisiana, to give birth to her child. At the time Louisiana adoption laws were known to be especially lenient. Many of the babies born and brokered through Louisiana were slated for New York clients by the infant entrepreneurs. Although the state of New York does not keep detailed statistics on out-of-state adoptions by its residents, in October 1987, John E. Strepp, deputy counsel for the State Department of Social Services, stated to the press, "We get more than an average number of children from Louisiana."[7] As of September 30, 1987, the Louisiana state legislature had revised the laws to make it illegal for an out-of-state mother and an out-of-state adoptive couple to go to Louisiana to arrange for the transfer of custody of a baby.

However, at the time, the expectant young Pennsylvania mother agreed to meet the baby merchant's demands and go to Louisiana. In return for her cooperation, she was offered round trip airfare, spending money, a new maternity wardrobe, and medical coverage for all expenses associated with the child's delivery.

When she was five months' pregnant, the young woman left her home without informing her parents of her intentions or destination. Neither she nor the individual with whom she had become involved had ever tried to obtain their consent for the adoption despite the fact that their daughter was still a minor.

The baby merchant had secretly arranged the expectant mother's travel plans. She simply picked up a prepaid airline ticket at Pittsburgh International Airport and boarded a flight to Baton Rouge, Louisiana. The entire operation had been arranged over the telephone. Prior to leaving Pennsylvania, the pregnant teenager had never met the man with whom she dealt.

When her parents realized that she was missing, they reported her disappearance to the Pennsylvania State Police. Fortunately the teenager was found five days later. The young woman's parents went to Louisiana and returned home with their daughter prior to her having given birth.

Judianne Cochran, director of Children's Rights of Pennsylvania, served as a member of a committee established by the Pennsylvania Attorney General's office, which became involved in the case after becoming aware of the possibility that other pregnant teens might have been secretly lured to Louisiana under similar circumstances. According to *The New York Times,* Ms. Cochran made the following comment regarding the intermediary/merchant involved: "Basically, we hope to put him out of business. We want to shut down the interstate network and transportation of juveniles."[8]

The arrest warrant for the individual involved charged him with enticing the pregnant Pennsylvania teenager to run away from home and specified that he violated Pennsylvania law by interfering with the custody of a minor and conspiring to publish misleading advertisements.[9]

The incident, through which a young woman and her unborn child were exploited, is representative of some of the typical tactics employed by those involved in supplying babies to others for high profits. As Jeff Rosenberg, director for adoption services at the Washington-based National Committee for Adoption, described the incident: "What we have here is literally a baby-chase mentality. I have had very legitimate couples tell me that they would do anything, literally anything to have a baby. It just builds, especially when they've gone through years of infertility treatments and they're getting older."[10]

At times unscrupulous physicians either may be actually involved in marketing children or may act as referral agents for the infant dealers. Often the young women whom they treat may tend to view their doctor as a respected authority figure. He may become a substitute father of sorts, or is seen as "someone who knows what's best for her," and has her best interests in mind.

An obstetrician, who also happens to be active in black market adoption, will usually continue as the young woman's physician throughout her pregnancy. The doctor will help her to deal with the pain of childbirth as well as assist in her recovery. And within a short period of time, if not immediately, the young woman's doctor will be someone whom she psychologically trusts.

A doctor involved in the sale of children will be prepared to supply a young pregnant patient with any number of reasons why she would be best off opting for independent adoption as opposed to working through a traditional adoption agency. The doctor may tell her of a wonderful couple who'd be just perfect for her baby. Or he could wonder aloud how she could give up her baby without knowing the people who'd be the child's new parents. He might also provide her with faulty information, telling her, for example, that if she used traditional channels, her baby would probably remain in foster care for over a year before being placed in a permanent home.

Although various techniques may be used, all are designed to be effective. Some obstetricians involved in black market adoption employ a sympathetic nurse or assistant whose office duties include making overtures regarding independent adoption to pregnant teens and young single women. The nurse may have perfected what sounds like a well-rehearsed sales pitch aimed at a vulnerable young person.

She may tell the young woman that she's very close to a wonderful couple who are unable to have children of their own. Perhaps she'll go on about how the couple had been promised a baby by another woman who cruelly went back on her word. (The implication is that the one to whom she's speaking would never take such unthinkable action.)

The nurse may elaborate to strengthen the scenario she's attempting to create. She might tell the pregnant teenager that the forlorn couple had already decorated the nursery for the baby. She may add that they had already purchased baby clothes, toys, furniture, a tricycle, or perhaps even started a savings account for the child's college education.

She'll do whatever she feels is necessary to paint a picture of a wealthy couple who badly want and need a child to complete their lives. A couple who can be assisted only by the lonely, troubled, and confused pregnant teenager at whom the nurse has directed her campaign.

However, in actuality, the couple described to the expectant mother may not exist at all. The young woman's baby may simply go to the highest bidder.

Often an unmarried pregnant teenager may feel alienated and isolated during what she may see as the most difficult and trying period of her life. In many instances the families of these young women have been less than supportive of their predicament. Under these circumstances a pregnant teen may be especially vulnerable to kind and seemingly well-meaning individuals who act as though they are pleased with her. Such a person may be too easily charmed and influenced by authority figures who have gone out of their way to shower her with positive attention.

There are a number of reasons why unmarried pregnant women elect to put their babies up for adoption. Many young women feel unprepared to take on the responsibilities of child rearing. As one such fourteen-year-old expressed her feelings: "If you were pregnant, fourteen, and had no way of supporting a baby, what would you do? I just got too much life ahead of me to be tied down with a kid. Just think, when I'd be twenty, the kid would be starting school. No way."[11]

Often mothers who give up their children do so because they believe it's in the child's best interests. They may feel that a prosperous married couple might be able to offer their baby advantages that would not be available to the child in a less affluent, single-parent environment.

In some cases choosing adoption may allow an unmarried mother finally to resolve a highly emotional issue. She may reason that once her baby is placed in the best possible home, she'll be free to go on with her own life. Even though she may never be able to erase the memory of her child, she'll feel assured that her baby is being well cared for elsewhere.

Many young women opt for independent adoption because it may superficially appear as the best alternative. Often homes for unwed mothers may still be stereotypically viewed as punishment hideaways where pregnant females are expected to live out their term of shame.

A mother who puts her baby up for adoption may think that she's permanently separated from her child, but in independent adoptions, this may not always be the case. For example, Connie, a teenager from Dayton, Ohio, didn't realize she was pregnant until it was too late to have an abortion.[12] Through friends, she contacted a New York attorney who promised that her baby would go to a good home and that she'd be financially assisted with her medical expenses.

As Connie recalled, "The child would get a really good education, be able to go to college, and, you know, have everything. . . . He [the lawyer] described the procedure. When I left the hospital, I would take the baby—I had to do it—it was the law that I take the baby downstairs and give it to him and he would give it to the people."[13]

Connie met the attorney for the first time only in the hospital after she had given birth. When she handed her child over to him, the adoptive parents remained in an adjoining room so that Connie never met them. Connie hoped that now she'd be able to go on with her own life. She and her mother decided not to mention the infant again.

However, as it turned out, things didn't go as planned. Nine months later Connie received a registered letter from the attorney who had arranged her child's adoption. A portion of the letter read: "I've been informed that 'boy' [Connie's last name] has been brain damaged since birth and that condition has only been discovered recently. My clients have abandoned all intention of adoption and custody after learning about his illness. The child is presently in New York Hospital in New York City. You have the right to reclaim the child. Please communicate with me immediately."[14]

The news deeply shocked and upset Connie's family. According to Connie's mother, "It was the most horrifying letter I've ever gotten in my life. It was like they were talking about a piece of damaged merchandise, not a human being; that we had given them damaged goods and they wanted us to come and pick them up. We had no previous warning that there was anything wrong until we received the letter. When Connie read the letter, she became completely hysterical."[15]

Connie, who had begun to resume her life as a normal teenager, now faced a renewed nightmare. As she recalled, "The first thing I thought was that we should go and get him and bring him back to Dayton to take care of him. But at that point I felt helpless to do anything. I wasn't financially capable of taking care of him, and I guess every mother feels a little guilt of 'What did I really do? What went wrong?' I thought maybe if I had kept him he might have been normal. I didn't know what to do. I wanted to help him."[16]

Actually Connie and her mother were more than surprised to find themselves in the circumstances they were now in. They had questioned the attorney about just this sort of thing prior to signing the final surrender papers. However, at that time the attorney had done his best to assure them that if such an event should occur, the adoptive parents would retain custody of the child. As Connie recalled, "It would be their problem. Those were his exact words."[17]

Connie had now been forced to face a painful dilemma. After some careful thought, she realized that she'd never be able to provide for and take care of the baby. The child became a ward of New York City.

Pregnant women who become the victims of baby merchants are rarely if ever given the actual facts regarding the process they are entering into. Often they are supplied misinformation or are deliberately lied to. If the pregnant female suspects that something is amiss and questions the attorney or dealer, she may be threatened into remaining silent.

One woman who believed that her attorney had unduly profited from her child's adoption found it useless to complain. According to her, ". . . the lawyer only gave me two hundred dollars. I was gonna complain, but he said not to mention getting any money. He said they could put me in jail if I mentioned it."[18]

At times baby merchants have resorted to using prostitutes as a product supply source of sorts. In her book *Baby Selling: The Scandal of Black Market Adoptions*, Nancy Baker reports that Nevada brothel owner and operator Joe Conforte was approached for this purpose by two attorneys from Oklahoma.

The men told Conforte that they'd be willing to pay up to ten thousand dollars a child for babies born to prostitutes employed by him. However, according to the brothel owner, due to the birth control pill and the availability of abortions, he knew of no such infants for sale.[19]

At times certain women have agreed to have a baby for profit as an alternative to the drudgery and hard work of prostitution. Usually these women demand a high price for the service they provide. There are attorneys in several states in the East who show prospective adoptive parents photographs of both men and women and allow their customers to preselect the parents of the baby whom they'll eventually purchase.[20]

For the most part babies who serve as commodities for marketeers are usually the children of impoverished and/or frightened and confused young women. This may be partly due to the fact that these expectant mothers are easier to find than professional baby breeders. In addition baby merchants dealing with troubled young women facing a difficult predicament may find the situation advantageous to their profit margin. These mothers may be unaware of the substantial sums being paid for their children. They may believe that the person assisting them is acting only in the child's best interest. Often they don't even realize that their baby has been sold.

FIVE

INFANTS
FROM OVERSEAS

Discouraged by the dearth of available infants in the United States, some people have sought to adopt from abroad, but this is not the answer for everyone. Some couples who wish to adopt have expressed anxiety over their ability to successfully raise a child who might be accepted within their family but rejected by others. As Elsa Eisenberg, founder of the Latin American Parents Association, stated in an article in *McCall's* magazine, "There are people who are not good candidates for children who are not going to resemble them and they shouldn't adopt these children. Other people are flexible. It's what feels right for you." [1]

The path to foreign adoption is not always easy, even for those who feel comfortable adopting a child of a different background. Foreign adoption can be risky and laden with roadblocks and red tape even under the best of circumstances. And, unfortunately, unscrupulous baby brokers have not neglected this supply source as well.

*This four-year-old Vietnamese boy
enjoys his first American Christmas after
being adopted by an American family.*

When dealing with unethical intermediaries, the results can be disastrous. Countless thousands of dollars have been lost by couples dealing with disreputable attorneys who either could not locate a child for them or were unable to secure an exit visa for the child from its country of origin.

Couples wishing to adopt foreign-born children are generally advised to work only through a reputable source. But even under the best of circumstances, adopting a child from another country may prove to be a harrowing experience. A case in point was the experience of Pat and Gary Janco, a Florida couple who tried to adopt a child from Honduras.[2]

At first things seemed to go along well enough for the Jancos, who had worked with a Miami agency. After keeping them waiting for a year, the agency had informed them that an eighteen-month-old girl named Caroline had been abandoned in a mountain hut in Honduras. The Jancos decided that they'd take the child sight unseen, and they told their lawyer to proceed with the arrangements.

A week later Pat and Gary Janco were informed that little Caroline had an eight-month-old sister. They were asked to take the baby as well. Since the cost of the process amounted to about fifteen thousand dollars per child, at first the couple wasn't sure they'd be financially able to bring both girls to the United States. However, as they didn't want to separate the sisters, the Jancos managed to raise the necessary amount.

Although foreigners who wish to adopt Honduran children are usually required to remain in the country for four weeks, the Jancos were instructed to stay in Honduras for just two weeks. Following their brief stay, they were told to return to the United States for an additional two weeks, and then fly back to Honduras to pick up the girls.

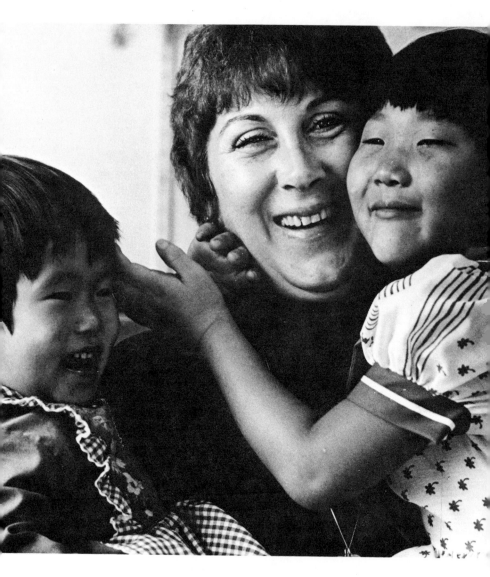

*Lorri Kellogg (center) spent thousands of
dollars to adopt her Korean-born daughters.
She then founded Florida's first agency
dealing solely with foreign-born adoptions.*

Things did not go as smoothly as planned for the couple. Initially their trip was postponed from November to December due to complications that were not revealed to the Jancos. When they finally arrived in Honduras, their lawyer met them at the airport and then escorted them to a dingy, dirty hotel room.

In a *Cosmopolitan* magazine article, Pat described their first meeting with the children as follows: "About seven that evening, the lawyer knocked at the door, shoved two children at us, and left. The babies were filthy, sick, and wearing only soaked diapers made of rags. Maria (the eight-month-old) was dangerously thin—just thirteen pounds—and couldn't even sit up." In the same article, her husband Gary added, "We'd fallen in love with them instantly, so that didn't change our decision to take them at all."[3] After the two sisters were medically examined, it was determined that both girls were severely malnourished and that the younger girl might be brain damaged as well.

But the Jancos' adoption difficulties were not over. At first inept court translators nearly had the Honduran officials thinking that the Jancos were the ones who had originally neglected the sisters. Fortunately, Pat Janco's minimal Spanish skills, along with the efforts of an able translator, helped matters along.

Later the couple went on a somewhat reckless four-hour ride through the mountains in order to be interviewed by a social worker. As Ms. Janco recalled, "The lawyer, driving like a madman, got so close to the edge that we thought we'd fall over. Parts of the dirt road were washed away by the rain and we crossed crevices so wide we could see straight down."[4]

After meeting the approval of the social worker, the Jancos flew back to the United States as planned. Although they had expected to return for the girls after two weeks, they were not permitted back until nine weeks had passed, due to delays in the Honduran courts. As little Maria had been so sickly, they feared that her health might deteriorate further, but there was nothing they could do.

Once the couple returned to Honduras, there were still more problems to face. Somehow the police had been wrongly informed that the Jancos were involved in black-marketing babies. Their lawyer was arrested and held overnight by the authorities. However, since the Jancos could prove that the girls' adoption was legal, all charges were dropped, and their attorney was released.

Despite their many mishaps, the Janco story did have a happy ending. Their two adopted daughters now enjoy a warm and loving home. Not all adopted children from foreign countries share their good fortune, though.

Some children are blatantly sold. For example, a Mexican mother and daughter team, who had acted as the key dealers in a baby-smuggling ring, were uncovered by the U.S. Immigration and Naturalization Service. The ring, which had operated from an unlicensed home for unwed Mexican mothers near Tijuana, had allegedly received as much as ten thousand dollars a child.[5]

The two baby dealers were arrested in San Diego, California, after having handed over a five-day-old infant to Phil and Linda Phillips of Kalama, Washington. The American couple had agreed to cooperate with the authorities after learning that the daughter they had adopted earlier was actually an illegal alien. The Immigration and Naturalization Service permitted the Phillipses to retain custody of their daughter since they had believed that their child's adoption was legal.[6]

Numerous other couples, who had innocently believed that their children were legally adopted, had inadvertently been duped by the child-smuggling ring. According to authorities, the ring had operated in eight states from New York to California, with the exact number of babies sold still unknown.[7]

In recent years El Salvador has also proven to be a fertile hunting ground for black marketeers involved in the illegal abduction and adoption of infants and young children. The relative ease of the adoption procedure in El Salvador, the country's recent civil war, and the extreme poverty and hardship known to its people have contributed to making the country one of the mainstays for foreign adoption in the hemisphere.

One woman, who had just been released from the hospital after giving birth to a baby boy, had her day-old child snatched out of her arms as she paused to cross the street on her way home. In less than an instant, a strange man had surged past her, grabbing the infant. The young mother screamed out in horror, but it was too late. The kidnapper had already escaped with the child.

When the woman turned to the authorities to try to retrieve her child, she was informed by family court officials that little could be done for her as they had no way of tracing the child's whereabouts. As one attorney present stated, "It probably went the way of other babies and was sent to the United States."[8] Formally, court officials in El Salvador described the incident as part of what Minister of Justice Julio Samayoa referred to as the "scandalous and alarming" black market abduction of their country's children.[9]

Due to the tremendous foreign demand for infants and very young children, child profiteers have flagrantly engaged in fraud, the falsification of documents, and widespread kidnapping throughout the Central American country. The vast majority of these children go to the United States, as it appears that not only is the demand for infants greatest there, but the potential adoptive parents are also willing to pay the highest prices for children.

According to foreign diplomats and Salvadoran officials, some unscrupulous lawyers have established illegal but profitable networks in order to procure infants for foreign adoption.[10] They've turned adoption into a lucrative business by hiring scouts to locate and coerce desperately poor young mothers into surrendering their children for adoption. In addition, they've paid other individuals to procure the false documents necessary for the children to exit the country. They've even set up makeshift nurseries in which to house the children during the interim.

It has been roughly estimated that each year the hundreds of El Salvadoran adoptions transacted have yielded over a million dollars in inflated agent and lawyer fees alone.[11] According to United States consular officials, some Salvadoran attorneys regularly pay kickbacks to their contacts or agents in the States.

Several of these American agents or "baby facilitators," as they've been referred to, are being investigated by the United States Immigration and Naturalization Service. In addition the government of El Salvador has also ordered an investigation and has stated that it intends to tighten its adoption regulations and procedures. As Carmen Barahora, the Deputy Interior Minister, stated in *The New York Times,* "We plan to make it harder to adopt. We are not against adoption, it can do a lot of good. But what's going on is terrible. We don't want children used for business."[12]

In Zacamil, a run-down public housing project located on a hillside area north of the city, young mothers speak nervously about the possibility of losing their young to kidnappers. A common complaint is the lack of police protection in the poorer villages. Some mothers who have attempted to solve the problem have had to resort to keeping their children indoors most of the time.

In the *New York Times* article, two sisters from the housing complex described how a strange man wielding a gun had approached them demanding that they surrender their infants to him. However, when one of the children screamed and tried to get away, the kidnapper panicked and fled.[13]

The article went on to describe the preventative measures taken by Naomi Escobar, a young merchant owning a small store in the area. As a mother Ms. Escobar feared that her very young children might unintentionally leave the safety of her yard while playing. In order to protect them, she wove a web made of twine across the bars of her gate. She hoped that the barrier might stop them from slipping through the bars and out of her sight.[14]

Ms. Escobar had tearfully described to the press how a young, well-dressed man had approached them in a seemingly friendly manner. However, when she turned her back for a moment, the stranger had tried to run off with her three-year-old daughter.[15] Fortunately, a neighbor who had witnessed the attempted abduction screamed loudly, calling attention to the kidnapper and aborting his efforts.

It is not uncommon to find baby merchants roaming the villages, refugee camps, and city slums of El Salvador in search of salable human merchandise. In one refugee camp, a woman said a stranger had come into the camp and convinced some of the women to give up their babies.[16] He told them that he had a close friend who would place the children in good homes in an affluent country where they'd enjoy a comfortable life. However, in actuality, the true fate of these children remains unknown.

If a couple in the United States wishes to adopt a child from abroad, the Immigration and Naturalization Service requires that they produce a written consent form for adoption and immigration. The prospective adoptive parents must present the written consent to the American consulate in the country of the child's birth in order to obtain an exit visa for the infant. In addition a birth certificate and a health certificate for the child must accompany the form.

Anyone involved in an adoption procedure who knowingly falsifies the circumstances surrounding the child's birth either by altering the immigration documents or by lying to the authorities is in violation of U.S. immigration laws. However, in the article in *The New York Times,* an attorney considered reputable by the United States Consulate indicated that such chicanery is common in adoption dealings of this nature. According to the lawyer, "Once you have a child, it's easy to falsify the papers. A woman is asked to pose as the mother, and she gets a birth certificate. Then the false mother signs a paper consenting to the adoption."[17]

In response United States Consul officials have stated that they've begun to scrutinize visa applications leading to adoptions more thoroughly. The government of El Salvador has stated that it intends to tighten its adoption regulations as well. Nevertheless, the U.S. consulate in El Salvador has reported that it continues to handle more visas for adopted children than most other ports.[18]

Unfortunately, an unsavory international traffic in children still thrives as well. In such situations kidnapping rings supply children not only for illegal adoption, but also for prostitution, mutilation, and murder. According to Renée Bridel, a Swiss U.N. delegate in Geneva who prepared a comprehensive report on the international traffic in children, "This involves hundreds of thousands of children from all over the Third World. . . . They are sent to wealthy countries everywhere, including the United States and Canada."[19]

Those who deal in the sale of children employ various strategies to secure their illegal commodity. At times these children may simply be snatched off the streets. In a number of instances, poor illiterate parents, living in countries where the average daily income is less than a dollar, were told that their children would be fed, housed, and educated by a relief agency.

While these parents were initially assured that they'd be able to visit their offspring as often as they wished, when they attempted to do so, they found that no such educational institutions had ever existed.

They were horrified to learn that they'd be unable to recover their children. It was later found through an investigation that the nearly blank documents trustingly signed by these parents were actually forms through which they'd relinquished their children for adoption.[20]

According to a United Nations report, tens of thousands of children have become the victims of flesh peddlers. Some have been illegally sold overseas for exorbitant sums to anxious would-be parents. Others have met devastating fates. Information from the United Nations indicates that some children are illegally sold to beggars' syndicates. Often these children

*Thousands of children—even as young
as two years old—have been sold and
used in pornographic videos.*

are deliberately mutilated in order to make them appear more pathetic, and in this way increase their possible earning potential.[21]

As one doctor who had an opportunity to treat some of these unfortunate children described the situation, "I have examined a number of these beggars, who are put out each morning with the syndicate and collected, with their earnings, in the evenings. Some have severe malformations of the limbs which are not the result of congenital problems, but have been acquired by binding up the limbs for a long period. I also found that these injuries were surprisingly similar. It's as if somebody learned how to do a certain amputation and just went ahead doing it like an assembly line."[22]

Still other children who escape disfigurement may be sold into brothels or exploited as models in pornographic films and magazines.

According to a U.N. investigator, "Begging doesn't really bring in the big money. Pornography does. The biggest income comes from very young children, down to the ages of two- and one-year-olds. They are filmed and photographed in acts of pedophilia and even with animals. You can buy these cassettes all over the world and play them at home. And there are even films now on the market in which underage girls are actually put to death. From what I know these films are made by gangsters in the United States, Hong Kong, and Manila and are screened in the United States and South America."[23]

SIX

THE LARGER PROBLEM

The sale of infants and children for adoption and other purposes remains a shocking reality. Human beings are often sold for the highest dollar, and yet there appears to be little being done about the practice. It is rare to hear that a baby broker has been indicted, and convictions of individuals involved in the trade are even scarcer.

Baby selling is difficult to stop or even to control. In an effort to circumvent American adoption laws, at times unscrupulous baby brokers have resorted to securing quick Mexican adoptions for their clients. Although adoption proceedings in the United States may take up to two years, a Mexican adoption may be finalized in under an hour.

A Mexican adoption bypasses all the bureaucratic red tape usually associated with adoption. A study of the prospective adoptive parents' home by a social worker is not required as it is in the United States. An in-depth itemization of the attorney fees for ser-

This Chinese peasant woman offered to sell her daughter to reporters.

vices or the moneys paid to the biological mother need not be submitted for scrutiny by the Mexican courts. In a Mexican adoption proceeding, the infant's natural mother doesn't even have to appear in court personally in order to relinquish her rights to her child.

Attorneys and others involved in the brokering and sale of children may resort to Mexican adoptions for their clients living in states in which independent adoptions are outlawed or where the legal requirements seem especially cumbersome. In order to arrange for a Mexican adoption, the U.S. attorney must supply the Mexican court with a birth certificate for the child from the state in which the infant was born. Special power of attorney forms must also be obtained to enable a Mexican attorney to act on behalf of both the American natural mother and the adoptive parents in court. In addition the adoptive parents must also supply two character references.

Once a Mexican judge approves the adoption, it takes about two to three weeks for the final decree to be issued. The Mexican attorney then sends the certified adoption papers to the adoptive parents' U.S. attorney. A Mexican adoption is recognized as legal and binding in the United States.

The American attorney presents the decree to the Department of Health in the state in which the infant was born. A new birth certificate will be made up for the child. The new document will show the name given to the child by his or her adoptive parents and will list the adoptive parents as the child's natural parents. Since the infant's original birth certificate is permanently sealed by the Mexican courts, there is no evidence that any adoption ever took place.

The amended birth certificate, which erases any trace of the adoption proceedings, makes it impossible for a U.S. agency to investigate the adoptive parents who become involved in Mexican adoptions. The Mexican courts can rely only on the written character affidavits supplied by the adoptive couple themselves. These court officials have no real way of actually knowing whether these glowing testimonies were bought and paid for. In some instances, the results have been disastrous for the children involved.

At times, some Mexican adoptions have been challenged. For example, in 1976 the New York State Department of Health refused to issue an amended birth certificate listing the adoptive parents' names to an American baby adopted in Juarez, Mexico, by a Long Island, New York, couple.[1] In this case, the New York State Department of Health charged that the Mexican court that had finalized the adoption had not had the proper authority to do so. Still, when the case was brought to court, the presiding judge sided with the adoptive parents. The court determined that the health department's duties in issuing a new birth certificate were merely of an administrative nature. And the judge ordered the department to proceed with the paperwork. However, the health department appealed the verdict. Eventually, the New York State Court of Appeals overturned the lower court's ruling.[2]

As a result of the state's Supreme Court ruling, infants born in New York with adoptions processed in Mexico will no longer receive amended birth certificates.[3] Since the New York verdict, several other states have begun similar actions in cases involving infants born in their states who were adopted by American parents outside of the country. However, child merchants are nevertheless reluctant to forsake this lucrative outlet for their dealings. To circumvent such restrictions, they need only arrange to have the infant's natural mother give birth in a state that recognizes Mexican adoptions.

Part of the problem inherent in ending the profitable baby trade lies in the fact that there is no national adoption law that is uniformly applicable across America. Each state has its own adoption laws, and often tremendous variation exists.

Despite the fact that many areas now have statutes to prevent profiteering from the sale of infants and children, often these restrictions contain substantial loopholes. At times the laws may be vaguely worded, leaving the roles and duties defined for individuals involved in placing children for adoption difficult to interpret precisely.

In fact in some instances the laws may be so ambiguous that the only time a baby merchant's activities come to the attention of the authorities is when individuals who have collected exorbitant sums from the prospective adoptive parents have failed to deliver the child promised to the couple. Whenever possible, baby merchants make certain that the courts never see a full disclosure of the actual moneys exchanged. So if a case eventually goes to court, it becomes extremely difficult for a jury to distinguish between an infant's selling price and the intermediary's legitimate legal fee.

In addition baby merchants are well aware of the differences in state laws, and use the variations to their advantage. They may consider it practical to involve a minimum of two to three states in each of their transactions.

For example, they may arrange for the birth mother and the prospective adoptive parents to live in different states. If necessary, the infant's biological mother might be sent out of state when she is about to give birth. If the adoptive parents live in a state which prohibits independent adoption, the individual orchestrating the adoption may advise them on setting up a residence in a more permissive state.

Prosecutors who try to tackle baby-selling cases face other obstacles as well. In order to piece together the various parts of the crime puzzle, it is necessary to positively identify the numerous parties involved. The infant's identity, as well as the names of the natural mother, the natural father, the adoptive parents, and the broker who acted as the intermediary, must be ascertained. Baby merchants who rely on interstate dealings as well as on securing false identification for the natural mothers make this a formidable task.

To worsen the situation, all adoption records in this country are sealed by court order. This is to protect the privacy of the parties involved in the adoption. However, this also serves to make it extremely difficult for prosecutors to identify victims as well as illegal intermediaries. A district attorney who lacks the testimony of both the adoptive parents and the natural mother and who is unable legally to obtain even minimal information regarding the details of the adoption will be hard pressed to build a strong case against the child merchant in question.

Even when the various parties involved in the adoption have been identified and located, they may not prove to be cooperative witnesses. Adoptive parents, who may have paid a tremendous sum for the child of their dreams, may actually be grateful for the opportunity to have done so. The baby broker may have afforded them their only viable chance for a family of their own, and if things went well, they are not about to turn him in.

In fact in numerous instances attorneys in the baby

Phil and Linda Phillips worked with federal immigration officials to crack a baby-smuggling operation that sold an estimated two hundred infants to U.S. couples. They are holding counterfeit paperwork and the five-day-old baby girl who was sold to them for $4,000.

business have secured more than one adopted child for the same couples. These people do not consider themselves victims. In fact, when a baby merchant is brought to trial, the couples are often extremely reluctant to reveal the true nature of their arrangements. Instead of speaking against him, they may ironically prove to be the child merchant's best character witnesses.

The infant's natural mother may be reluctant to expose the baby merchant as well. She may hesitate to come forward because she does not want to expose herself as having had an illegitimate child. And if she were afforded a bit of extra cash by the intermediary, she may fear that she'll be criminally prosecuted along with him.

In some cases the child's natural mother didn't realize initially that her baby was being sold. She may now wish to testify voluntarily against the broker who took the child. Nevertheless, the prosecutor handling the case may still have to overcome tremendous obstacles.

Even though the natural mother may be cooperative, the child's adoptive parents may remain unknown. Their identities are protected through the sealed adoption records of their home state. Courts in different areas of the country vary in their readiness to open these records for the purpose of an investigation. And this factor inadvertently acts to impede criminal inquiries.

Even when a court of law orders that the adoption records be opened, the prosecutor's efforts may still be thwarted by other regulations which go hand in hand with this action. For example, some states, such as New York, require that if the adoption records are opened by court order, the adoptive parents must be immediately notified. Therefore, if they purchased their baby for an exorbitant price, they are afforded an opportunity to destroy any financial records or documents which might reveal the true nature of the transaction.

The fact that more than one state may be involved in a black market adoption also makes jurisdiction a problem for prosecutors to contend with. A grand jury subpoena has legal force only within the borders of the state from which it's issued. And frequently the cooperation between states in bringing witnesses before each others' grand juries tends to be especially lax. Comparable jurisdictional difficulties also hamper the prosecutor's ability to secure important court records and relevant bank documents.

The fact that those involved in black market adoption usually use more than one state in their transactions also makes it especially costly for prosecutors to pursue investigations. For example, if a case comes to the prosecutor's attention in which the natural mother lives in Oregon, the attorney is from New York, and the adoptive parents are from Michigan, the travel expenses of the prosecutor's legal staff will soar in order to pursue the various leads involved and conduct the necessary interviews.

A district attorney's office has to operate within a fixed annual budget. In choosing to pursue cases, any such office will be forced to consider the priorities of the local constituency. This means that black market adoptions have to compete with murder cases and other high visibility crimes for time and funding.

Even when black market adoption cases are tackled, they are difficult to win. Part of the problem lies in the fact that many baby merchants are actually licensed attorneys. And in a number of states these individuals have effectively used their credentials to defend their exorbitant fees.[4]

However, even when a prosecutor has been able to assemble all the vital pieces of a case effectively, it may still be extremely difficult to obtain a conviction. Even an excellent case may fall on the deaf ears of an apathetic public and court system. Unfortunately, often people do not view black market adoption as a crime. Conscious of the fact that there is a scarcity of white infants, the public may feel that the shortage justifies the high fees required. Too frequently, the public is prepared to believe that if the baby went to a good home, no real crime was committed, regardless of the cost.

Sadly, this attitude is perpetuated even by the very courts whose obligation it is to put a stop to the sale of children. As Elizabeth Cole, director of the North American Center on Adoption, stated in the book, *Baby Selling*, "Not taking this seriously is a problem all through the black market situation. Many judges think there's nothing wrong with this. This is a nice couple, so what? Maybe they paid a little money for the youngster, but they can afford it. They would have paid it for a vacation, or a trip around the world, or a house, but they'd like a child more, so what's the harm? They just look the other way because they don't think it is serious business."[5]

In addition to the potential danger to an infant who's been bought and sold and to the young naive natural mothers duped in these transactions, at times the adoptive parents may become the baby broker's victims as well. Frequently they are lied to about the baby's health and genetic background. Years after the adoption has been finalized, they may learn that the child suffers from an inherited health condition that had not been immediately visible at birth.

Still other victims of black market adoption include the thousands of potential adoptive parents who are either too ethical to seek out a baby merchant or are simply unable to afford the high fees. With black marketeers scooping up available white infants, couples who have already met the requirements of traditional agencies may find themselves on the waiting lists for a significantly longer period of time. On a broader societal level, the sale of infants may actually deprive some suitable potential adoptive parents of their only opportunity for a family, while innocent children continue to be strategically merchandised.

SEVEN

——————— $ ———————

SURROGATE MOTHER CONTRACTS

The scarcity of babies available for adoption has resulted in the development of any number of new methods by which childless couples can begin a family of their own. Among the most controversial to arise in recent years is that of surrogate motherhood.

In most instances a surrogate mother is a woman who is paid to have a baby for another couple. Usually, she'll be artificially inseminated with the sperm of a man whose wife is infertile or unable to carry an infant to term. After the surrogate gives birth, she immediately surrenders the child for adoption to the couple who paid her to perform this service for them.

Surrogacy and its implications have become a highly charged emotional issue in America. For many couples who may be faced with the reality of remaining childless throughout their lives, surrogacy is a positive solution to a difficult dilemma. Others see surrogate motherhood as a commercial baby-breeding scheme run by intermediaries who are actually the newest wave of baby merchants.

Mary Beth Whitehead, herself a surrogate mother,
believes surrogacy is "a form of brainwashing." She
works with the National Coalition Against Surrogacy.

The majority of intermediaries who match surrogates with prospective adoptive couples are attorneys, although there are a number of physicians who are actively involved in the business, and commercial surrogate centers exist as well.

According to Phyllis Chesler in her book *Sacred Bond: The Legacy of Baby M,* "Sperm donors, inseminating physicians, and businessmen comprise an industry that caters to infertile men and their wives."[1] She goes on to describe the involvement of a well-known attorney in contracting surrogate mothers as follows: "[He] thought it was a great idea. However, under the law, cash payments were illegal; initially he recruited volunteers. [The attorney] was able to arrange only five surrogate births. He took a three thousand dollar 'finder's fee' for each one. [The attorney] knew that in order for surrogacy or contract motherhood to become an industry, women would have to be paid and contractually bound. He and other lawyers began to examine the loopholes and publicize the 'cause.' Positive media coverage would insure that even if contracts could not be enforced, surrogacy profiteers would not be criminally prosecuted as baby sellers."[2]

Sacred Bond paints a picture of surrogate motherhood as actually being little more than a well-oiled business largely run by men for profit: "Lawyers, physicians, and other business people have organized the surrogacy or contract-motherhood industry into 'clinics' or 'programs.' They are essentially business companies. The company lawyer and the administrative staff represent the contract father. Their job is to insure that the contract father gets his genetic child and that the contract mother (the surrogate) does not. . . . The company recruits or screens the contract mothers. The inseminating physician may be a partner in the company or part of the company's lucrative business network."[3]

The issue of fees paid for surrogate services is often a problematic area for intermediaries involved in the process. The Thirteenth and Fourteenth Amendments to the Constitution outlawed slavery and guaranteed equal protection to all under the law. A baby, or any human being for that matter, may not be purchased at a predetermined price contractually agreed to by participating parties.

Supposedly, the surrogate mother is not selling her infant. The surrogate brokers instead argue that surrogate mothers are merely being paid for the services they perform in the production of a human product. In other words, the money received by a surrogate mother is earned by her for carrying and giving birth to the baby, rather than for the infant itself.

However, if this were really the case, a surrogate mother could make significantly more per hour working in a fast food restaurant while avoiding all the risks and discomfort inherent in pregnancy and childbirth. As cited in the book *Sacred Bond:* "If the surrogate is not being paid for the baby, but only for her gestational 'services,' then, according to state law, she is being grossly and illegally underpaid; i.e., she is not earning the minimum wage per hour; nor is she being paid in cash or on a weekly basis. If, on the other hand, a 'surrogate' is being paid to surrender the baby (a 'product'), then the contract violates both state and federal laws against baby-selling and against peonage or indentured servitude; i.e., a citizen and human being cannot be forced to perform against her will; nor can she be jailed for refusing to 'specifically perform.' For example, no one can force a football player to 'play ball' or an opera singer to 'sing' against his will once he's quit—even if he's contractually promised to do so."[4]

Currently, a woman who wishes to become a surrogate mother may simply answer a newspaper ad which offers $10,000 to have the baby and provides a phone number to call. A prospective surrogate mother will then meet with an intermediary who will act as a broker of sorts throughout the process. Often, she'll be given a physical examination by a physician and a brief interview with a psychologist or social worker. At times the psychological interview to determine if the woman will be able to act successfully as a surrogate and relinquish the child will be omitted.

Although the intermediaries who arrange surrogate agreements would like their clientele to think that a careful and thorough screening process is applied to all applicants, this is hardly the case. While candidates for surrogate motherhood are supposedly required to meet rigid standards as ascertained through extensive interviews and testing, in actuality such conditions rarely exist. In fact some clinics are so anxious for business that they'll send surrogate mother applicants to any number of psychologists until they come up with the positive response they are looking for.

A case in point is that of the surrogate mother who is now serving a life sentence in an Oregon prison after shooting her three young children without apparent cause. One child died as the result of her rampage, while the other two remain permanently paralyzed. Such incidents raise the issue of how thorough the psychological evaluation performed on this surrogate could have been.

Another surrogate mother who was initially a strong proponent of the process and later became disillusioned by her experience described the psychological testing aspect of surrogate mother programs as follows: "I am appalled at the lack of proper counseling, before and after the pregnancy. There are (also) no requirements for the psychological testing of the prospective parents."[5]

If a woman is accepted as a suitable candidate for surrogate motherhood, her photograph and a brief biographical sketch are left with the agency to be viewed by potential takers. There are no requirements for couples wishing to hire a surrogate other than the ability to pay both the surrogate's and the intermediary's fee, along with related expenses. Some surrogate agencies request that prospective customers submit a report from their doctor certifying that they are in good health and are infertile, but most do not do this. Stringent requirements and careful screening would limit the intermediary's potential range of customers.

The couples interested in using the services of a surrogate mother will leaf through the pictures and biographies of the available women. Usually they'll identify two or three who interest them and then meet with the women to determine their final choice.

After the couple has selected the woman, the attorney or institute will usually draw up a contract to carefully outline or delineate the obligations and duties of the various parties involved. The contract is considered essential to make certain that the infant's natural mother will immediately surrender the child at birth and in no way attempt to retain custody and thereby block the subsequent adoption procedure.

In most instances a typical contract will generally specify that the woman acting as the surrogate mother will be impregnated with the sperm of the male of the couple through artificial insemination. After the infant's birth, the child will be turned over to the couple who paid for the surrogate's services.

In return the couple hiring the surrogate is financially responsible for all the surrogate's medical and related expenses not covered by the surrogate's own insurance plan. In addition, the surrogate mother will be paid a separate fee once she has successfully fulfilled her part of the agreement. Usually the fee paid to a surrogate mother is about ten thousand dollars, although at times higher amounts may be negotiated. This fee is retained in an escrow account administered by the attorney or intermediary involved, and is not released to the surrogate mother until all the terms of the contract have been satisfied.

In addition to the contract existing between the couple and the surrogate mother, the lawyer-intermediary will also draw up a separate contract defining the scope of his relationship to his clients or the adoptive couple. This is done largely for the lawyer's own protection and to insure that his personal interests are safeguarded regardless of what later transpires between the surrogate and the couple.

The contract between the attorney and the adoptive parents specifies that the lawyer will still be paid his fee by the couple regardless of whether or not the surrogate actually ever becomes pregnant or adheres to the terms of the contract.

As the practice of commercial surrogacy has become more widespread, charges of exploitation have arisen. One woman recounted her experience as a surrogate mother this way: "Before I was inseminated, they tested me for everything. Turns out they didn't test Ben (male of the contractual couple) very carefully, only for AIDS and syphilis. His sperm gave me a sexually transmitted virus. I had an infection for two months. Maybe nobody thought a man would have a disease. He was a professor. They just thought that he was perfect."[6]

At times the unprofessional and dishonest treatment imposed on their clients by surrogate brokers extends to the adoptive couples as well. A number of intermediaries have been sued by their clients. The Gannett News Service reported that one lawyer dealing in surrogate arrangements has been sued by nearly a dozen of his clients.[7] In *Sacred Bond* author Phyllis Chesler also described several such incidents as cited in the publication *New Republic:* "One surrogate underwent artificial insemination before any contract had been signed. Another was approved despite a history of heart disease; in two other cases, the surrogate mother bore her husband's child—not the client's."[8]

Still another case involved a twenty-five-year-old Michigan woman whose previous medical history had been ignored by the attorney who wished her to act as a surrogate mother. The woman had recently been operated on for cervical cancer. In addition, the woman had experienced five miscarriages out of nine previous pregnancies.[9]

In some instances, lonely unattached young women with unrealistic expectations may volunteer to become surrogate mothers. Unfortunately brokers anxious to earn their commission may encourage these women to act on their feelings despite their obvious emotional unsuitability. As Debbie, a young surrogate mother, expressed her motives, "[I thought] if I had a baby for somebody, they would help me with the rest of my life. I know that sounds awful, but I just thought I'd have a relationship with these people all my life. Harriet [adoptive mother] said that I'd always be with them on holidays. I told my son that I was going to have a baby for Ben and Harriet and that the baby would be like a cousin to him. He would always be able to see it, play with it, grow up knowing the baby."[10]

However, after the infant was born, it wasn't long before Debbie realized that she and her older son were not going to be part of the baby's new family. Although many couples who use the services of a surrogate mother are grateful to the woman for giving them a child, they frequently tend to shun the child's natural mother following the infant's birth. Often these women may now be viewed as intruders whose possible claim to the baby might threaten the unity of the newly formed family.

Just as when pregnant women who have promised to give up their children for adoption experience a change of heart and are threatened by their baby brokers, under similar circumstances surrogate mothers may be subject to the same type of intimidation.

A young surrogate mother told of her broker's reaction when she first mentioned that she might have made a mistake in signing the contact:

The broker threatened me. He said they'd make things really hard for me to keep my baby. He didn't get explicit. But I know he'd threatened other surrogate mothers. One surrogate said he had threatened to get her husband fired. Another surrogate said this guy could make your life absolute hell. He'd have a battery of lawyers against you. He'd make sure you had to pay every penny back or get you into jail if you couldn't pay it back fast enough. The broker told me that he had a hunch that I was on welfare and that he was going to check the county welfare records and report me for trying to earn money as a surrogate if I backed out of the deal.[11]

Some surrogate mothers have fought to retain custody of their babies in spite of the odds against them. Laurie Yates, the surrogate mother of twins, is one such woman. Laurie and her husband Rich had hoped to have a child of their own, but unfortunately Rich's low sperm count prevented them from doing so. The couple thought about using a sperm bank, but the costs involved proved to be prohibitive.

Laurie saw surrogacy as a means through which she'd eventually be able to have a child with her husband. She'd use her surrogate fee to later cover the sperm bank's costs. As she said in a recent magazine article, "If I delivered a healthy baby, I would receive ten thousand dollars. I had never thought of surrogacy, but ten thousand dollars would certainly solve our problem. If I spent nine months having a baby for someone else—and nine months didn't seem like such a long time—Rich and I would receive enough money to have our own baby."[12]

Ms. Yates and her husband decided to go through with the plan, and Laurie was soon accepted as a surrogate. Although the young couple didn't fully comprehend the legal ramifications of their actions, they went ahead with the process. According to Ms. Yates: "I can't say that we truly did understand all the legal and medical terms, but we were so pumped up with enthusiasm for what we were doing and so sure that [our attorney] was our savior that we didn't hesitate a minute."[13] Her husband Rich added, "I had to sign reams of papers like these when I joined the navy."[14]

Although Laurie Yates had fully intended to relinquish the child (she had twins) when she signed the papers, her feelings changed during the pregnancy: "When I was totally at rest, I could feel the first stirrings of the babies within me. I concentrated on them. I thought of them as tiny human beings, growing from my eggs, coming into the world, then growing up. How would they feel years from now, if they learned that their real mother had given them up—for money? The thought was unbearable, so unbearable that I knew I had my answer. I made my decision. The babies inside me were mine, and I had to keep them." [15]

Laurie Yates, along with her husband, fled from the couple who had contracted for her services as a surrogate mother as well as from the lawyer who had acted as the intermediary throughout the procedure. She and her husband hid out in a house in Ithaca, Michigan, which her family owned but hadn't lived in for years. It was a stressful and financially difficult period for Laurie and her husband, but she remained determined not to turn over her children. "We were at the end of our rope. Rich loaded our furniture into a rented truck, and we drove to Ithaca [between Lansing and Mt. Pleasant] where my folks had a house that hadn't been lived in for two years. My dad told us that we could stay there for a while. We would have to go on welfare to eat, but the house would save our lives. At that point, neither [the contractual couple] or the [lawyer-intermediary] knew where we were." [16]

In the meanwhile Laurie attempted to reach Connie Binsfeld, a Michigan state senator, who had introduced an anticommercial surrogacy bill into the state legislature. As Ms. Yates described her efforts in an article in *Good Housekeeping* magazine, " 'Please help me,' I begged the person who answered the phone in her office. I'm a surrogate mother, I'm pregnant with twins, and I'm in hiding because I don't want to give up my babies." [17]

The legislator's aide suggested that Ms. Yates find an attorney to represent her. Laurie was fortunate in locating a team of attorneys who not only were aware of the legal ramifications of surrogate contracts as a woman's issue but also were sympathetic to Ms. Yate's dilemma. They agreed to take on her case.

One attorney, who was only three years older than Laurie Yates, informed the surrogate mother that it was against Michigan law either to sell a child or to consent to an adoption prior to that child's conception. The attorney went on to explain that federal law prohibits selling a bodily organ and suggested that renting or selling a woman's womb for the express purpose of producing a child might be regarded as a violation of that statute.

During this period Glenda and Barry Huber, the couple who had contracted Laurie Yates to act as a surrogate, became aware of her whereabouts. The lawyer-intermediary from the surrogate center had filed a "notice of claim for paternity" in a county court on the couple's behalf.

Shortly thereafter the Hubers arrived at the Yateses' door. Unfortunately their arrival came at a difficult time for Ms. Yates, who had been in and out of the hospital due to several incidents of premature labor. Ms. Yates was too tired and ill to talk to the couple. Mr. Yates answered the door and politely requested that they leave.

With the passage of time, the twins, Anthony and Stephanie, were born. When they were a week old, Laurie Yates had them baptized in her home. Four days afterward, at a hearing at the Ithaca, Michigan, courthouse, a judge granted the biological father and his wife the right to a weekly two-hour visit with the twin boy and girl.

*Richard Yates comforts his wife Laurie
as she testifies before a House subcommittee.
Mrs. Yates urged the House to pass
a bill outlawing surrogacy.*

For the first three months of the childrens' life, the babies remained with Laurie and her husband most of the time. Each week the Yateses took the babies to the home of Evelyn Green, the children's court-appointed supervisor, for a visitation period with the Hubers.

When the children were a few months old, the court extended the Hubers' time with the babies, granting them "expanded visitation." This meant that each month the Hubers had the twins for two weeks and the Yateses had them for two weeks. Each couple was permitted visitation rights on alternate Saturdays. In order to be closer to the children, the Hubers rented a house near the Yateses' residence in Michigan.

Since acting as a surrogate mother, Laurie Yates and her husband have tried to warn other couples of the pitfalls inherent in such arrangements. They went to Washington to testify before the House Commerce Subcommittee in support of a proposed bill to outlaw commercial surrogate agreements.

Although Laurie Yates and her husband regret the circumstances surrounding the twins' birth, they are delighted with the children. As Laurie Yates said in an interview, "We are happy with our decision to keep them, because when they grow up and ask about their birth, we'll have a good answer. "We'll say— 'Mommy became pregnant with you because we needed the money—but we loved you too much to give you up.' "[18]

EIGHT

THE TRIANGLE TRAGEDY

Perhaps the most famous instance of a surrogate mother unable to give up her child is that of Mary Beth Whitehead Gould, in what subsequently became known as "the 'Baby M' trial."

On February 6, 1985, a twenty-eight-year-old housewife named Mary Beth Whitehead signed a surrogate mother contract with Bill Stern, a thirty-eight-year-old biochemist and his wife Betsy Stern, who was also thirty-eight and a physician. At the time Mary Beth Whitehead was the mother of an eleven-year-old boy, Ryan, and a nine-year-old daughter named Tuesday. The Sterns, who had contracted Mary Beth to act as a surrogate mother, had no children.

According to the agreement Mary Beth Whitehead was to be artificially inseminated with Bill Stern's sperm. After giving birth, if she legally surrendered the baby to Bill and Betsy Stern for adoption, she would be paid ten thousand dollars. If the artificial insemination was unsuccessful and Mary Beth Whitehead did not conceive, she would receive no compensation for her efforts. If Ms. Whitehead had a miscarriage or gave birth to a stillborn child, she'd receive one thousand dollars.

The contract between Ms. Whitehead and the Sterns was arranged through a third-party intermediary, The Infertility Center of New York (IFCNY). The attorney running the center was to receive $7,500 for his role. Therefore, in order to participate in the surrogate agreement, the Sterns had to pay a minimum of $17,500.[1] In addition they were required to pay medical expenses associated with Mary Beth Whitehead's pregnancy and the delivery of the child.

What the Sterns weren't aware of when they interviewed and subsequently selected Mary Beth Whitehead as their choice was that ten months earlier the center's own psychologist, Dr. Joan Einwohner, had expressed some reservations about Mary Beth Whitehead's "tendency to deny feelings." As reported in Phyllis Chesler's book, *Sacred Bond*, "Dr. Einwohner thought it would be important to explore with [Mary Beth] in somewhat more depth whether [Mary Beth] will be able to relinquish the child at the end. [Mary Beth's] husband Rick [a Vietnam veteran and sanitation worker] has had a vasectomy. [Mary Beth] may have more needs to have another child than she is admitting."[2] Unfortunately, Bill and Betsy Stern were never notified of the psychotherapist's findings.

The parties involved signed the surrogate mother contract, and on that very day a physician began the artificial insemination process. Mary Beth Whitehead did not conceive on the first try, and as a result she and Bill Stern, sometimes accompanied by Betsy Stern, returned to the sperm bank center for subsequent attempts.

The process was repeated nine times, until in July

1985, Mary Beth Whitehead had became pregnant with Bill Stern's child. At first things seemed to go along well enough. However, the smooth relationship that had initially existed between the Whiteheads and Sterns soon experienced difficulties. As time passed, Mary Beth Whitehead began to feel that Betsy Stern tended to use her credentials as a physician to unduly interfere in Mary Beth's medical care and relationship with her own doctor.

In November of 1985 the Sterns wanted Mary Beth Whitehead to undergo amniocentesis. Amniocentesis is a test designed to show birth defects in the fetus prior to birth. It allows the parents to generally assess the child's medical condition and determine whether they wish an abortion to be performed.

Mary Beth Whitehead didn't want the amniocentesis. However, she felt that she had to go along with the Sterns' wishes because the contract which she had signed prior to her pregnancy granted them this right. To worsen matters, Mary Beth Whitehead hadn't been well during the pregnancy. She had developed phlebitis, and as a result was bedridden for several weeks.

Her discomfort and anxiety were heightened by the beginning realizations that perhaps she had made a terrible mistake in entering into a surrogate mother pact. The new life growing inside her now caused Mary Beth to question her feelings and earlier resolve.

Meanwhile, the relationship between the Whiteheads and the Sterns continued to disintegrate. Even weeks earlier the Sterns had noticed that Mary Beth now seemed to withdraw from them.

Ms. Whitehead went ahead with the amniocentesis to comply with the Sterns' demands. But despite the fact that the test showed the child's sex in addition to giving other vital data, Mary Beth refused to reveal to the Sterns whether the child was a girl or a boy. Ms. Whitehead also decided against having the Sterns present with her in the delivery room.

On March 27, 1986, Mary Beth Whitehead gave birth to a baby girl at Monmouth Memorial Hospital in Long Branch, New Jersey. Her husband, Rick, was present with her at the birth. They thought that the new baby resembled their older daughter Tuesday. Mary Beth felt a strong attachment to the child. She doubted whether she'd be able to ever part with her baby for money or because she had signed a contract to do so. The child, who'd been part of her body, had become a precious part of her life, and she wanted to keep her new daughter.

Mary Beth and her husband named the baby Sara Elizabeth and filed a birth certificate which identified the infant as Sara Elizabeth Whitehead. Mary Beth began breast-feeding the baby and later took the child home with her from the hospital. She had her young daughter baptized in the Catholic church.

Bill and Betsy Stern were upset over Mary Beth's attachment to the child they'd hoped would be theirs. On Easter Sunday, only three days after the little girl's birth, they persuaded Ms. Whitehead to let them have the baby.

Mary Beth Whitehead tried to adhere to the surrogate contract and to understand what the Sterns were going through. However, she found that she was still unable to give up the child. She refused to accept the ten thousand dollars fee owed to her for acting as a surrogate.

After a tearful and sleepless night separated from her infant, Mary Beth begged the Sterns to return the little girl to her. Touched by her obvious emotional suffering, the Sterns temporarily gave the baby back to Mary Beth for what they believed would only be a few days.

But once the baby had been returned to her, Mary Beth found it impossible to surrender her daughter. During the next few weeks, there were numerous phone calls between the Sterns and the Whiteheads. Finally, on April 12, 1986, Mary Beth Whitehead informed Bill and Betsy Stern that she would not part with the child.

The Sterns sought legal help to regain possession of the baby. Their attorney, Gary Skoloff, petitioned the court for intervention, and on May 5, 1986, Judge Harvey Sorkow granted the Sterns sole temporary custody of the infant. When the judge issued the order, he hadn't yet met Mary Beth Whitehead. She hadn't had an opportunity to have an attorney represent her interests before the judge. To worsen matters, at the time at which the judge granted the Sterns temporary custody, the infant had already been breast-feeding for nearly six weeks.

Armed with a court order for the baby, the Sterns, along with the local police, arrived that evening at the Whitehead residence. However, the court order identified an infant girl named Melissa Elizabeth Stern, the name which the Sterns had given the child. When the police attempted to take the child, the Whiteheads showed them the baby's birth certificate which bore the name Sara Elizabeth Whitehead. Mary Beth Whitehead and her husband claimed that the police had no right to remove the child from the premises.

During all the confusion Ms. Whitehead carried the infant into the bedroom. There she handed the child through an open window to her husband. Carrying the infant in his arms, he quickly left the yard.

When the police realized that the child in question was gone, they arrested Ms. Whitehead. She was handcuffed and taken to the police station in a squad car. As there were no actual grounds for her arrest, she was later released.

In an effort to prevent the authorities from taking her baby, Ms. Whitehead and her family left their New Jersey home. They remained in hiding in Florida for eighty-seven days, staying for a portion of the time with Mary Beth's parents, Joseph and Catherine Messer.

It was an extremely difficult period for both the Whiteheads and the Sterns. Judge Sorkow had frozen the Whiteheads' assets, making it impossible for them to withdraw money from their bank account. In addition the bank had threatened to foreclose on the Whitehead's New Jersey home.

The Sterns knew that Mary Beth and the baby were somewhere in Florida. During their time spent in hiding, Mary Beth Whitehead made several desperate calls to Bill Stern, which Mr. Stern taped. The following is an exerpt from one such call:

MARY BETH: *Bill, you think you got all the cards. You think you could do this to people. You took my house. I mean, we don't even have a car anymore. I can't even afford the car payments. You took everything away from me. Because I couldn't give up my child? Because I couldn't give up my flesh and blood, you have the right to do what you did?* . . .

BILL: *What can I do to stop it, Mary Beth?*

MARY BETH: *Bill, I'll let you see her. You can have her on weekends. Please stop this.*

BILL: *Oh, God. I can live with you visiting. I can live with that, but I can't live with her having a split identity between us. That'll hurt her.*

MARY BETH: *What's the difference if I visit or if you visit? I've been breast-feeding her for months. Don't you think she's bonded to me?*

BILL: *I don't know what she's done, Mary Beth.*

MARY BETH: *She's bonded to me, Bill. I sleep in the same bed with her. She won't even sleep by herself. What are you going to do when you get this kid that's screaming and carrying on for her mother?*[3]

The stress experienced by Mary Beth Whitehead and her family while in hiding continued to mount. During this period Ms. Whitehead became ill with a severe infection and was admitted to a Florida hospital. Three days later, detectives armed with a court order to return the baby to the Sterns unexpectedly arrived at Ms. Whitehead's parents' Florida home.

The men pulled the baby from her crib while the infant's nine-year-old sister, Tuesday, screamed at them to stop as she hit one of the officers with her hairbrush. Meanwhile Bill and Betsy Stern had been waiting for the baby back at the Florida police station.

Judge Harvey Sorkow did not allow Mary Beth Whitehead to see her daughter again for five and a half weeks. Later on, in September of 1986, Ms. Whitehead was permitted supervised one-hour visits with her daughter twice a week. The sessions took place in a small room on state property in the presence of an armed guard and a nurse matron. Mary Beth Whitehead was forbidden to breast-feed the baby.

Then on January 5, 1987, the highly publicized courtroom battle which came to be known as the Baby M trial began. The trial to determine the baby's legal parents lasted almost eight weeks. During the proceedings nearly every aspect of Mary Beth Whitehead's past and personal life was scrutinized and attacked.

The differences in the two couples' backgrounds were emphasized as well. Mary Beth Whitehead had not gone past high school, and at the time of the trial was married to a sanitation worker. Bill and Betsy Stern, on the other hand, were professionals, both holding graduate degrees in the sciences. Betsy Stern is a pediatrician who had also earned a doctorate in human genetics.

When challenged in court by the Sterns' lawyer as to her qualifications to raise her daughter, Ms. Whitehead answered, "I don't have an education. I don't have a skill. The only skill I know I do well is that of being a mother. There's no limit to anything I'll do for my child."[4] As the trial continued, women's groups demonstrated outside the courthouse in support of Mary Beth Whitehead. They signed petitions as well as picketed, carrying signs which bore such slogans as "A Woman Doesn't Have To Be Perfect To Be A Mother," and "Sara Whitehead Is Her Name".

On March 31, 1987, Judge Sorkow delivered his 121-page decision on the Baby M case. The judge ruled in favor of the child's biological father, granting full custody to Bill Stern. The judge also terminated the parental rights of Mary Beth Whitehead, which meant she would no longer be permitted to see her daughter. In addition Judge Sorkow denied a request for visitation privileges from the baby's maternal grandparents.

In response Ms. Whitehead's attorneys legally challenged Judge Sorkow's decision. On April 10, 1987, the New Jersey Supreme Court agreed to hear Ms. Whitehead's appeal and granted her permission for a weekly two-hour visitation period with her daughter in the interim.

Finally, on February 3, 1988, the New Jersey Supreme Court announced its decision in the Baby M case. The court ruled that commercial surrogate mother contracts were both illegal and unenforceable in the state of New Jersey. Although Bill Stern retained custody of the child, Mary Beth Whitehead's visitation rights were fully restored.

Still another woman who came to regret her role as a surrogate mother is Elizabeth Kane (a pseudonym), the first-known paid surrogate in America. Ms. Kane, then a thirty-seven-year-old housewife and mother of three, decided to become a surrogate mother in order to help a childless couple. As she explained to her family in her book, *Birth Mother*, "Who cares if I know them or not? I want to do this for the childless couples of the world. For the pain and anguish our friends have suffered because they're infertile. You know what they've been through. You've seen it. If I can spare one couple that trauma, that's enough for me."[5]

At times during her pregnancy there were gnawing doubts, but she did her best to try not to think about the consequences. "The unexpected primitive urge to suckle a child was still there. Was I strong enough to remain detached and objective until this pregnancy was over? My maternal instincts were still strong. Would that mean trouble when it came time to give the baby away? Was the whole idea of being a surrogate mother a terrible mistake? I pushed these distressing thoughts deep into the back of my mind. I'd deal with them another time."[6]

Her surrogate pregnancy was not an easy period for either Ms. Kane's family or herself. Because of her actions, Ms. Kane's husband was unfairly fired from his job. She found that some people, whom she'd considered friends, now wanted nothing more to do with her. Her children were teased and taunted about the situation at school. And Elizabeth Kane herself began to have disturbing dreams.

> *I began having nightmares. Always the same one. I dreamed that I would emerge from a long, long labor exhausted and weak, drenched in sweat from the exertion of pushing the baby out of my body. At the moment of triumph, after the final barbaric cry from my throat and the first lusty one from my child, I held out eager arms, anxious to hold the warm, naked little body and put it to my breast.*

> *But in the dream there were other arms reaching for the child. Two nameless, faceless people waited while [the doctor] delivered the baby. When I was done, the three of them would celebrate his birth and toast his health, while I lay on the delivery table, legs still in metal stirrups. I was alone and lonely and my arms were empty.*

> *I always fought to wake up, and shivering and damp with perspiration, I would huddle under the quilts and ponder the foolish vision that might not be too far from reality."[7]*

While acting as a surrogate mother, Elizabeth Kane was the object of national publicity. Despite the fact that she was often tired and had three children to care for at home, the physician who acted as the intermediary in the process continually pressured her to do press interviews and television talk shows. As she cited:

> *I would complain when [the doctor] called to ask me to do "one more" publicity show for him. I wasn't receiving any financial benefit, while he seemed to be. His telephone would ring for days after I had done a show in another large city. The publicity generated more surrogates and drew more infertile couples to his doorstep, eager to open up their checkbooks to him. Sometimes I would resent his growing bank account, while Kent [her husband] and I struggled with our bills. I would not get paid until after the baby was born. Even then it would be several weeks before [the doctor] finally mailed me that check. As for the publicity, I never received one cent—nor did I want to—for all the traveling and speaking I did on behalf of surrogacy."[8]*

Seven years after surrendering the child she bore as a surrogate mother, Elizabeth Kane has become painfully aware of what she's referred to as "the ramifications of exchanging babies for dollars."[9] She now believes that surrogate motherhood merely transfers the pain from a woman who is unable to have children to a woman who will suffer the loss of the child she gave away.

Following the birth of the baby, Ms. Kane lapsed into a prolonged period of depression. She became obsessed with the infant's absence, and the reality that even though she knew where her young son was, she was unable to be with him.

Elizabeth Kane is not certain how long her depression lasted but estimates that it could have been anywhere between six and eighteen months. During that time, her interest in seeing her friends or in keeping up her appearance waned, and she spent most of her time at home. As she described some of her worst feelings: ". . . The depression soon grew into fantasies of my death. . . . I was a blight that needed to be removed. I planned and replanned my death, rational enough to want the end of my life in the cleanest, least expensive yet most effective method."[10]

As she fought against her negative feelings, the suicidal fantasies gradually ended. She took up aerobics and began to follow a sensible diet. Later on, when she lectured on the topic of surrogate motherhood at Wayne State University in Detroit, Michigan, she said, "Surrogate motherhood has nothing to do with logic, but everything to do with loving and caring and emotions. Stop treating us like we are a disposable uterus. You're tossing away our feelings with the placenta. We are not human incubators!"[11]

Unfortunately too little attention has been paid to the effects of surrogate motherhood on the half brothers and sisters of the infant created. While she was pregnant as a surrogate mother, when her own young son was at home and bored without a playmate, Elizabeth Kane thought to herself, "I'm giving away your brother. You have no one to play with, and I'm giving away your half brother. His only male sibling who could become as near and dear to him as any full-blooded brother could ever be. What made me think the child I carried would mean nothing to my children."[12]

She thought of all the things the boys might do together if they'd been able to grow up knowing one another—hunting, swimming, wrestling on the living room floor. She wondered if her son would one day resent her role as a surrogate mother when he was old enough to comprehend why he'd never known his brother.

Ms. Kane thought that perhaps her daughter Laura experienced the loss most acutely. One morning, shortly after the infant's birth, the young girl burst into tears at the breakfast table. Unable to eat the food in front of her, she cried, "I never got to hold my baby brother."[13]

As Ms. Kane described her response in her book *Birth Mother,* "In speechless terror I watched her thin shoulders shake. I knew I could try to deny he was my son. I had told the world he belonged to another woman. But Laura knew the truth. He is her brother. Nothing that is said or done can ever change that fact. They share the same blood, the same grandparents, and the same mother. I was unable to stand there and tell her she was wrong. I put my arms around her and held her against me as her tears dampened my bathrobe. There were no words. [The baby's] absence was like a death. We had to mourn it together."[14]

Unfortunately, as it turned out, Elizabeth Kane's son was not left unscathed by the loss of his half brother. At age eleven, his mother described him as "clinging, fearful, and plagued by constant nightmares."[15] He had also developed a fear of death and was unable to fall asleep easily if he even heard about the death of an unknown person on the news. Her son's behavioral problems were later analyzed by a child psychologist as follows: "Your son is undergoing classic symptoms of grief and loss. It's as though you gave birth to a dead child, came home empty-handed, and never mentioned the baby again. There was no funeral, no family grieving, and little mention of the loss of his brother."[16]

Ms. Kane described the overall effect of her experience on her children as follows: "I had no idea that my children would bond with their brother during the pregnancy or would spend years aching for the touch and sound of him. We all long to share a tiny piece of [the baby's] life."[17]

With time Elizabeth Kane did her best to cope with the results of her actions. However, when the surrogate mother controversy involving Baby M and Mary Beth Whitehead captured the public's attention, she couldn't help but react—"A burning rage spread through me as I read about her nightmare. My most dire fears of women proceeding unwittingly to join the ranks of surrogate mothers had come to pass in the form of Mary Beth Whitehead."[18] As she tearfully wrote to Ms. Whitehead, "So you fell in love with your baby, Mary Beth, and no one told you it would happen. Well, so did I. So do we all!"[19]

While Elizabeth Kane's "bitterness at the exploitation of young women by unscrupulous professionals eager for an easy dollar spilled onto the page,"[20] she knew that she had to fly to New Jersey to help Mary Beth Whitehead in whatever way she could. She filed an affidavit with Ms. Whitehead's attorney stating her belief that "surrogate motherhood should be banned nationwide, that the practice caused unexpected emotional damage to surrogate mothers and their families."[21] Having been a firsthand victim of the damage, to Elizabeth Kane, the "long-term ramifications of surrogate parenting contracts were no longer a mystery."[22] She also appeared at a press conference with Mary Beth Whitehead where she tearfully related to reporters how much she missed her son and how she had never fully recovered from losing him. She charged that surrogate motherhood was a terrible error.

Later on Elizabeth Kane became a member of the National Coalition Against Surrogacy. In October of 1987, she, along with other supporters, testified at a hearing in Washington, D.C., in favor of a bill to ban paid surrogacy. She described her group's purpose as follows: "We were there to tell Congress about the business of buying and selling human beings, and to reveal our personal distress at having been part of that business."[23]

Among the concerns raised by surrogate mother contracts is the role of the middlemen-profiteers who benefit most financially from these agreements. As Ms. Kane attests, "It is important to study the motives of the physicians and attorneys running surrogate parent clinics. They claim every couple deserves a chance to start a family with a newborn, and yet their exorbitant fees ($1,500 for an insemination which should actually cost $324) prohibit a majority of the infertile from hiring surrogate mothers."[24]

In many instances infertile couples are not made fully aware of the potential emotional hazards involved in asking a stranger to sign away her own flesh and blood in accordance with the terms of a contract designed by an attorney. Often the question—is it unnatural to ask a biological mother to totally disassociate herself from the life growing within her?—is left unaddressed. Yet in actuality the human element which is so easily disposed of by baby merchants is what eventually causes surrogate mothers to violate the terms of their contracts when they realize that they are unable to part with their children.

At times the cold cash values imposed on different aspects of the surrogacy situations may be easily likened to slavery. A prestigious surrogate mother clinic on the East Coast has a contractual policy in which the surrogate receives ten thousand dollars for a normal healthy baby, but if the baby is mentally or physically defective, she forfeits her fee.[25]

Her surrogate contract also provides that if she changes her mind and decides to keep the child, she is then obligated to pay the biological father twenty-five thousand dollars. It is especially ironic because if the woman readily surrenders the child, the value to its father is only ten thousand dollars.[26]

Although the intermediaries involved in the surrogate business often profess that they are interested in creating happy families and helping infertile couples, often their bottom line amounts to little more than a dollar sign. As expressed in the book *Birth Mother*, "Many reproductive engineers now in charge of surrogate parenting clinics refer to the baby as a 'product' or as 'an investment.' When a potential surrogate mother walks through the door of a baby broker's office, she is viewed as a healthy uterus worth so many thousand dollars. The fact that the clinic is paid by the infertile couple immediately, while the surrogate must wait until the birth, has never been questioned."[27]

In subtle ways baby merchants anxious to recruit potential child breeders may actively encourage surrogate mothers to break the law. According to Elizabeth Kane, "I am also concerned about the surrogates from one well-known clinic in the Midwest who are not advised to pay taxes on their fees. Our accountant researched the law and informed us that my fee was considered income. These surrogates are being paid in smaller amounts to avoid any questions by the IRS. They are following the advice of their baby brokers, some of whom are attorneys and ironically may be breaking the law as a result."[28]

Current surrogate mother practices fall into other grey areas of the law as well. For example, if a surrogate mother is a housewife and her husband is employed, his insurance coverage may in many instances be used to pay the bulk of the medical costs incurred. The couple contracting the surrogate are generally responsible for the medical expenses involved in the prenatal care and delivery not covered by the surrogate husband's plan. As a result, some insurance companies may be paying maternity benefits for men other than those who are actually covered by their policy.

Several insurance companies are now considering adding clauses to their policies to specifically exclude surrogate parenting situations. The issue of medical expenses becomes especially ironic when the surrogate mother is a welfare recipient. An affluent couple who contracts for the surrogate's services pays the intermediary a substantial sum, yet the majority of the baby's delivery costs will be subsidized by taxpayers.

Frequently women who become surrogate mothers act under the domination of the intermediaries or baby merchants who tend to exploit them for profit. As Phyllis Chesler commented in her book *Sacred Bond,* "The fanatical, almost stubborn naivete exhibited by these women is impossible to convey. Happy or unhappy, they took great pride in how they trusted and obeyed everyone blindly about everything. These women believed whatever the surrogacy-clinic lawyers and doctors told them. They rarely asked questions; they never disobeyed an order. They did exactly what they were told to do—and therefore couldn't 'believe' that they'd been used for 'one thing only'; that they 'never mattered,' i.e., that their fantasies of being 'above' it all had little to do with the realities of trafficking in women for profit."[29]

To a growing number of individuals, surrogate motherhood is an unacceptable alternative. According to Chesler, "It is immoral to buy and sell the flesh of a living human being for profit; to trade human organs (or whole humans) as if they were sugar, coffee, bananas. . . . The removal of a child from his birth mother—against her will and for profit—is even more heinous than the forced removal of a woman's kidney. A birth mother (her body and her mind) is connected to and remembers her missing baby."[30]

It has been argued that surrogate motherhood situations reduce the status of newborns to that of a highly tradable commodity, one that is reserved for individuals of means. The women who become surrogate mothers are usually significantly less well off financially than the people who hire them. Baby merchants can remain confident that often such women lack the monetary resources to engage in a lengthy legal battle if they change their minds and want to keep their children. These women have been referred to as a new class of breeders, and to some, surrogate motherhood amounts to little more than "reproductive prostitution."[31]

To a woman facing financial difficulties, ten thousand dollars may seem like a great deal of money. However, unfortunately, surrogate motherhood comes with its own set of problems.

Although a number of states have proposed laws to ban surrogate motherhood, as of yet only Louisiana and New Jersey have statutes to prohibit commercial surrogacy. These laws mean that the individuals who arrange surrogate mother agreements now have a somewhat more limited arena in which to operate. However, as they continue their profitable businesses, they may do so at the cost of the birth mother, her family, and the new life which they negotiated to create.

As one psychiatrist commented on the effects of surrogate motherhood, "And what of the child itself? When it learns the truth, how will it deal with the knowledge of a mother who gave it away for pay? And how can it have access to family medical history or be guaranteed a good home? Conventional adoption requires record keeping and careful selection of the adopting parents. Reproduction without sex does not."[32]

NINE

SOLUTIONS

What can be done about the black market in adoption? Some people believe that outlawing private adoption and commercial surrogate mother contracts on a national level would effectively halt the activities of baby merchants. As long as these activities are banned in only a few states, individuals continue to conduct their business in more permissive states.

There are persuasive arguments against ruling out private adoption as an alternative. Currently, private adoption affords the natural mother an option through which she can in some way participate in her child's future. If private adoption were outlawed, a natural mother who actually knew of a couple whom she wanted as her offspring's adoptive parents would be prevented from selecting them. Such a law would also seriously hinder the efforts of nonprofit religious or civic groups who have launched special projects to facilitate the placement of older, handicapped, minority, and other difficult-to-place children.

It has also been argued that legitimate private placements, which have nothing to do with the activities of baby merchants, may not be any less effective than traditional agency placements. According to a Child Welfare League spokesperson, "An agency professional, no matter how well trained and experienced, cannot be sure ever that a couple will make good parents. A social worker forms professional antennae to screen out the blatant crazies. I think that this happens with a responsible practitioner, even a lawyer."[1]

In addition, in a legitimate private adoption the attorney is largely responsible only for the court documents and other legal paperwork. Ideally, it is the task of a court-appointed social worker to determine the suitability of the adoptive parents.

When private adoption is handled ethically by responsible and caring individuals, there are many positives associated with it. The infant immediately goes to its new home following birth. One avoids the sometimes lengthy stay in foster placement while a traditional adoption agency selects proper parents. The infant is therefore afforded an opportunity to begin bonding with his or her new parents from the start.

Among the best arguments for not putting an end to independent adoption is that it might serve only to worsen the current situation. A procedure can be outlawed, but that doesn't mean the demand for a given commodity will be lessened. Couples who desperately want children and who've been turned away by traditional agencies will still try to find ways to become parents. If independent adoption were banned, baby merchants would be driven underground, where their business would now be conducted without any restraints or checks and balances whatsoever. The misrepresentation of facts as well as the prices would soar, leaving prospective adoptive parents with little or no legal recourse.

Resolving the current adoption crisis in the United States might be possible, but not without a thorough reevaluation of both traditional agency procedures and the independent adoption process. In addition individuals wishing to adopt need to rethink their values and their motivations behind their desire to parent. As was indicated earlier, many couples still blindly search for an infant. Most often their dream may be of a healthy white baby who will somehow magically mature to resemble them in every way.

Given the present baby shortage, couples might do well to reevaluate their selection criteria. Although a healthy white infant might be viewed by some as the American ideal, there are older children as well as children with physical and/or emotional problems who sorely need parents and a stable home. Flexible couples may come to realize that parenting these children brings a whole special set of rewards in addition to the knowledge that they may have provided a home for a young person who otherwise might have grown up parentless.

Although adopting what may be viewed at times as an "unwanted child" can be a rewarding solution for some couples, not everyone is willing immediately to take this step. In such instances some couples have found it beneficial to volunteer as foster parents for these special children. Such an alternative affords couples an accurate taste of what the day-to-day reality of parenting a special or older child might entail. And in some instances children in foster care can be legally adopted later by their foster parents.

As Reuben Panner of Los Angeles's Vista Del Mar Child Care Service suggested,

There is a tremendous need for foster parents, but it's really misunderstood. When we suggest that a couple become foster parents, they often reject the idea because they say the child will just go back to his own parents and they couldn't take that. But some people have been foster parents for years, and they're obviously getting a lot out of it. It's very rewarding to see a child grow, develop, become independent and go back to his family, then repeat the process with a new child. Besides, that's what happens with our own biological children. If we raise them correctly, they grow away from us and leave us.[2]

Ideally, traditional agency adoptions should be available to all applicants with a couple's suitability determined on an individual basis rather than measured against rigid guidelines. In addition traditional adoption agencies might also offer prospective parents a variety of helpful services that could include supplying them with information on alternatives to adopting an infant. As Lynne McTaggart suggests in *The Baby Brokers*, "The best of agencies would open its doors to all applicants, would provide prospective adoptive couples with information about all the children available to them, and would help them to discover whether they are best suited to an infant, a foreign child, a toddler, or an older child. . . . a home study would be done by a trained psychologist, who would be more qualified than a social worker to make the distinction between human frailty and psychopathology."[3]

It would also be extremely helpful to prospective adoptive parents if traditional adoption agencies worked together in forming a national computer base of available children. Whenever possible, orphaned and abandoned children from abroad could be included to afford adoptive parents as many options as possible.

If independent adoption is to survive as an effective option, both state and federal legislation to regulate it must be adopted. These laws would empower courts to delve more fully into the circumstances surrounding the adoption petitions brought before them. The roles of attorneys and other intermediaries involved in an independent adoption would also be more clearly defined. A scale of reasonable fees for an attorney's services in an independent adoption would be established, and referral agents would not be permitted to collect a fee for sending an expectant mother to an attorney for the purpose of pursuing a private adoption. Private adoption reform would include a provision to insure legally that the biological mothers receive objective professional counseling as well as be made fully aware of all the various options available to them.

It is certain that changes in the law and procedures, as well as in public opinion, will be necessary before any real difference can be made. If there are solutions, they aren't simple ones. But how can we continue as a nation in which children are priced and sold in a marketplace?

SOURCE NOTES

CHAPTER ONE

1. *New York Post,* 24 November 1987, p. 3.
2. *New York Post,* 24 November 1987, p. 3.
3. *New York Newsday,* 5 November 1987, p. 3.
4. *New York Newsday,* 12 November 1987, p. 29.
5. *New York Newsday,* 11 November 1987, p. 23.
6. Ibid.
7. *New York Newsday,* 11 November 1987, p. 3.
8. *New York Newsday,* 14 November 1987, p. 3.
9. *New York Newsday,* 11 November 1987, p. 23.
10. *New York Newsday,* 20 November 1987, p. 5
11. *New York Newsday,,* 12 November 1987, p. 3.
12. *New York Post,* 2 February 1989, p. 16.
13. *New York Post,* 21 November 1987, p. 1.

CHAPTER TWO

1. Anna Quindlen, "Baby Craving," *Life* (June 1987): 23.
2. Diane Salvatore, "Babies For Sale," *Ladies' Home Journal* (July 1986): 59.
3. Ibid.
4. Quindlen, "Baby Craving."

5. Sue Browder, "The Joys and Trials of Adopting Abroad," *Cosmopolitan* (May 1986), 270.
6. Ibid.
7. Bolles, Edmund Blair, *The Penguin Adoption Handbook* (New York: The Viking Press, 1984), 37.
8. Salvatore, "Babies for Sale."
9. Browder, "The Joys and Trials of Adopting Abroad."
10. Ibid.
11. Bolles, *The Penguin Adoption Handbook*.
12. Salvatore, "Babies for Sale," 60.
13. Ibid.
14. Mary Kuntz, "Paying Expenses Is Legal, Buying Babies Is Not." *Forbes*, 31 December 1984, p. 130.
15. Elizabeth Ehrlich, "Is Private Adoption Too Private?" *Business Week*, 14 December 1987, p. 106.
16. Ibid.
17. *New York Newsday*, 6 November 1987, p. 35.
18. Nancy C. Baker, *Baby Selling: The Scandal of Black Market Adoptions* (New York: Vanguard Press, 1978), 41.
19. Ibid.
20. Ibid, 42.
21. *New York Newsday*, 6 November 1987, p. 35.
22. *U.S. News and World Report*, 19 May 1975, p. 34.

CHAPTER THREE

1. *New York Post*, 2 February 1989, p. 16.
2. Diane Salvatore, "Babies for Sale," *Ladies' Home Journal* (July 1986), 63.
3. Ibid.
4. Ibid.
5. Lynne McTaggart, "The Booming Adoption Racket," *Saturday Review*, 10 November 1979, p. 15.
6. Ibid.
7. Lynne McTaggart, *The Baby Brokers: The Marketing of White Babies in America* (New York: Dial Press, 1980), 78.
8. Ibid, 79.

CHAPTER FOUR

1. Nancy C. Baker, *Baby Selling: The Scandal of Black Market Adoptions* (New York: Vanguard Press, 1978), 50.
2. Ibid, 51.
3. Ibid, 52.

4. Ibid, 53.
5. Ibid, 54.
6. *The New York Times,* 29 October 1987, p. B1.
7. Ibid.
8. Ibid.
9. Ibid.
10. Ibid.
11. Baker, *Baby Selling,* 56.
12. Ibid, 61.
13. Ibid.
14. Ibid.
15. Ibid.
16. Ibid.
17. Ibid.
18. Ibid, 64.
19. Ibid, 65.
20. Ibid, 66.

CHAPTER FIVE

1. Maryann Bucknum Brinley, "The Baby Business," *McCall's,* (June 1985), 140.
2. Sue Browder, "The Joys and Trials of Adopting Abroad," *Cosmopolitan* (May 1986), 272.
3. Ibid.
4. Ibid.
5. *Time,* 9 September 1985, p. 45.
6. Ibid.
7. Ibid.
8. *The New York Times,* 17 December 1985, p. 4N.
9. Ibid.
10. Ibid.
11. Ibid.
12. Ibid.
13. Ibid.
14. Ibid.
15. Ibid.
16. Ibid.
17. Ibid.
18. Ibid.
19. Cheryl McCall, "An Angry Doctor Battles Gruesome Black Market in Asian Children," *People Weekly,* 17 December 1981, pp. 46–50.
20. Ibid.
21. Ibid.

22. Ibid.
23. Ibid.

CHAPTER SIX

1. Lynne McTaggart, *The Baby Brokers: The Marketing of White Babies In America* (New York: Dial Press, 1980), 291.
2. Ibid, 292.
3. Ibid.
4. Nancy C. Baker, *Baby Selling: The Scandal of Black Market Adoptions* (New York: Vanguard Press, 1978), 122.
5. Ibid, 128.

CHAPTER SEVEN

1. Phyllis Chesler, *Sacred Bond: The Legacy of Baby M* (New York: Time Books, 1988), 54.
2. Ibid, 55.
3. Ibid.
4. Ibid, 113.
5. Elizabeth Kane, *Birth Mother* (New York: Harcourt Brace, 1988), 287.
6. Chesler, *Sacred Bond*, 61.
7. Ibid.
8. Ibid.
9. Ibid.
10. Ibid.
11. Ibid, 62.
12. Laurie Yates, "Don't Take My Babies From Me," *Good Housekeeping* (March 1988), 183.
13. Ibid, 186.
14. Ibid.
15. Ibid, 188.
16. Ibid.
17. Ibid, 189.
18. Ibid, 190.

CHAPTER EIGHT

1. Phyllis Chesler, *Sacred Bond: The Legacy of Baby M* (New York, Time Books, 1988), 3.
2. Ibid, 4.
3. Ibid, 6.

4. *Asbury Park Press,* 15 March 1987, p. 4A.
5. Elizabeth Kane, *Birth Mother* (New York: Harcourt Brace, 1988), 22.
6. Ibid, 91.
7. Ibid, 138.
8. Ibid, 58.
9. Ibid, 275.
10. Ibid, 278.
11. Ibid, 279.
12. Ibid, 194.
13. Ibid, 279.
14. Ibid, 280.
15. Ibid.
16. Ibid, 281.
17. Ibid, 290.
18. Ibid, 283.
19. Ibid.
20. Ibid.
21. Ibid.
22. Ibid, 284.
23. Ibid, 293.
24. Ibid, 286.
25. Ibid, 287.
26. Ibid.
27. Ibid, 289.
28. Ibid, 288.
29. Chesler, *Sacred Bond,* 47.
30. Ibid, 12.
31. Kane, *Birth Mother,* 285.
32. Ibid, 298.

CHAPTER NINE

1. Lynne McTaggart, *The Baby Brokers: The Marketing of White Babies in America* (New York: Dial Press, 1980), 329.
2. Nancy C. Baker, *Baby Selling: The Scandal of Black Market Adoptions* (New York: Vanguard Press, 1978), 172.
3. McTaggart, *The Baby Brokers,* 332.

$

FOR FURTHER
READING

"Adopting Babies From Abroad." *Money* v. 14 Oct 1985 p. 167 (1).
"After Baby M., Motherhood Not for Sale." *U.S. News & World Report* v. 104-Feb. 15 1988 p. 11 (2).
"As Adoptions Get More Difficult" by Harold R. Kennedy. *U.S. News & World Report* v. 96 June 25 1984 p. 62(1).
"The Baby Business" by Maryann Ducknum Brinley. *McCall's* v. 112 June 1985 p. 88(4).
"Baby Craving: Facing Widespread Infertility, a Generation Presses the Limits of Medicine and Morality (Special Report)" by Anna Quindlen. *Life* v. 10 June 1987 p. 23(4).
"Baby Farm; A Luxury Adoption Business" by Wendy Smith. *Time* v. 120 Aug 4 1988 p. 40(1).
"Babies For Sale" by Diane Salvatore. *Ladies' Home Journal* v. 103 July 1986 p. 58(5).
"Birth-Marketing," *Commonweal* v. 114 Dec. 4 1987 p. 692(1).
"Borrowed Bodies" by Susan Agrest. *Savvy* v. 8 Jan 1987 p. 52(4).
"Buying and Selling Babies: Limitations on the Marketplace" by Michael Novak. *Commonweal* v. 114 July 17 1987 p. 406(2).
"The Case of the Breach-of-Contract Baby." *Newsweek* v. 108 Sept. 1 1986 p. 66(1).
"Childless Couples Seeking Surrogate Mothers Call Michigan Lawyer Noel Keane—He Delivers" by James S. Kunen. *People Weekly* v. 27 March 30 1987 p. 93(4).

"Contracts and Apple Pie; the Strange Case of Baby M" by Katha Pollitt. *Nation* v. 244 May 23 1987.

"Desperately Seeking Baby: Ten Million Americans Are Struggling to Have Children" by Lewis J. Lord. *U.S. News & World Report* v. 103 Oct. 5 1987 p. 58 (6).

"Dilemma in Swaddling Clothes; Surrogate Mothers, Natural Fathers, and Baby M" by Judith Levine. *Harper's* v. 274 April 1987.

"Experts Differ on Visitation Rights in Baby M Case" by Robert Hanley. *The New York Times* v. 137 March 31 1988 p. 13.

"The Foreign Connection" by Mary Kuntz. *Forbes* v. 134 Dec 31 1984 p. 11.

"Hagar and Her Sisters: Precedent for Conduct: Surrogate Motherhood in the Bible" by James Gaffney. *Commonweal* v. 114 April 24 1987 p. 240(3).

"How Can Government Encourage Adoption?" *Christianity Today* v. 31 Oct 2 1987 p. 53(2).

"I Had to Pay Another Woman to Have My Baby." *Good Housekeeping* v. 202 April 1986 p. 32(3).

"Infantpreneurs (ethical aspects of private adoption service)." *Commonweal* v. 112 April 18 1985 p. 228(2).

"Infertility: Babies by Contract: Despite the Cost and Controversy, Childless Couples Turn to Surrogate Mothers" by David Gelman. *Newsweek* v. 106 Nov. 4 1985 p. 74(3).

"Is The Womb a Rentable Space? An Emotional Court Case Centers on Surrogate Births" by Richard Lacayo. *Time* v. 128 Sept. 22 1986 p. 36(1).

"Is There a Wrong Way to Make Babies?" (alternative methods of conception, birth, and the Catholic church) by Maureen Orth. *Glamour* v. 85 Oct. 1987 p. 61.(2).

"Invasion of the Body Snatchers" (human fertility manipulation) by Barry Richards. *New Statesman* v. 110 July 5 1985 p. 23(3).

"The Legal Angle: New Birth Technologies—From Artifical Insemination to Surrogate Mothers—Have Spawned a Host of Complicated Legal and Moral Issues" by Marion Asnes. *Vogue* v. 175 Aug. 1985 p. 327(2).

"Motherhood Not For Sale!" by Shelley Roberts. *Reader's Digest* (Canadian) v. 128 Feb. 1986 p. 77(2).

"The Paradox of Birth Technology; Exploring the Good, the Bad, and the Scary" by Ann Snitow. *MS.* v. 15 Dec. 1986 p. 42(5).

"Protecting the Liberty of Pregnant Patients" by George J. Annas. *New England Journal of Medicine* v. 316 May 7 1987 p. 1213 (2).

"The Religious and Moral Issues; Is Artifical Insemination a Form of Adultery? Is Paying a Surrogate to Carry a Child the Same

As Buying a Baby?" by Leslie Tweeton and Donna Scaglione. *Boston Magazine* v. 77 June 1985 p. 193(3).

"San Diego: Babies For Sale" (Mexican babies). *Time* v. 126 Sept. 9 1985 p. 45(1).

"Supreme Court Says No to Surrogacy for Pay" by Richard Lacayo. *Time* v. 131 Feb. 15 1988 p. 97(1).

"Surrogate-gate." (surrogate motherhood) (editorial) *Commonweal* v. 114 Jan. 30 1987 p. 35(2).

"Surrogate Motherhood: A Legal Labyrinth." by Ellen Wright Clayton. *USA Today* v. 116 Nov. 1987 p. 68(2).

"They Get a Baby, She Gets $10,000" by Leslie Tweeton. *Boston Magazine* v. 77 June 1985 p. 136(7).

"Want Ad Babies" (independent adoption) by Ann Chase. *Washingtonian* v. 22 Aug. 1987 p. 102(13).

"Where Have All The Babies Gone? Social Trends Have Made Adoption Impossible for Many Childless Couples" by Kelsey Menehan. *Christianity Today* v. 20 Oct 18 1985 p. 26(4).

"William Stern vs. Mary Beth Whitehead" (includes related articles on similar cases involving young children) by Andrea Fine, Kim Hubbard and Mary Shaughnessy. *People Weekly* v. 27 March 23 1987 p. 50(5).

"Womb for Rent" (surrogate motherhood) by Kathleen Rockwell Lawrence. *Vogue* v. 177 July 1987 p. 84(1).

"Wombs for Rent" (surrogate mothers; 1987: the Year In Science) by Patricia Gadsby. *Discover* v. 9 Jan. 1988 p. 64(1).

"Wombs Shouldn't Be for Rent" by Mary Meehan. *U.S. Catholic* v. 52 Sept. 1987 p. 16(6).

INDEX